CRÊPES, SOUFFLÉS & SNACKS

THE KITCHEN LIBRARY

CRÊPES, SOUFFLÉS & SNACKS

Gwyneth Loveday

OCTOPUS BOOKS

CONTENTS

This edition published 1989 by
Octopus Books Limited
a division of the Octopus Publishing Group
Michelin House
81 Fulham Road
London SW3 6RB

© Cathay Books 1983
ISBN 0 7064 3844 2

Printed by Mandarin Offset in Hong Kong

INTRODUCTION

As a food, eggs are unique. They are rich in protein, iron and vitamins, economical and easily stored.

When it comes to cooking, nothing is more versatile than eggs. They make cakes rise, soufflés light, batters crisp and custards set. Many great culinary achievements – such as mayonnaise and meringue – would have been impossible without them. As a cooking aid they are vital: for glazing pies and scones, binding croquettes and beefburgers, coating fish and fritters, clearing consommés and jellies, enriching pastry and thickening sauces.

Many of the recipes in this book are traditional classics, but there are some new ones too, and you're sure to find them all really cracking! Full cooking instructions for the basic recipes, such as omelets and pancakes, are given in the chapter introductions and should be referred to before starting on a recipe.

NOTES

Standard spoon measurements are used in all recipes
1 tablespoon = one 15 ml spoon
1 teaspoon = one 5 ml spoon
All spoon measures are level.

Size 3 eggs should be used unless otherwise stated.

Fresh herbs are used unless otherwise stated. If unobtainable substitute a bouquet garni of the equivalent dried herbs, or use dried herbs instead but halve the quantities stated.

Use freshly ground black pepper where pepper is specified.

Ovens should be preheated to the specified temperature.

For all recipes, quantities are given in both metric and imperial measures. Follow either set but not a mixture of both, because they are not interchangeable.

Eggs are now graded according to the following gram weights:

Size 1	over 70 g	*Large*
Size 2	65–70 g	
Size 3	60–65 g	*Standard*
Size 4	55–60 g	
Size 5	50–55 g	*Medium*
Size 6	45–50 g	
Size 7	under 45 g	*Small*

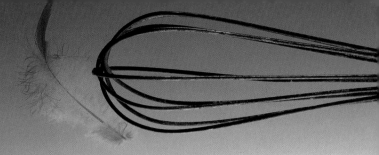

Simply Eggs

Soft-boiled Eggs: Make sure the eggs are at room temperature; very cold eggs may crack when they touch the water. Completely immerse the eggs in gently simmering water, cover and bring quickly back to simmering point. Cook for the following times: sizes 1 and 2, 3¾ minutes; size 3, 3½ minutes; sizes 4 to 7, 3 minutes.

If the eggs crack, add 1 to 2 teaspoons salt to the water to prevent the egg white seeping out.

Hard-boiled eggs: Completely immerse the eggs in cold water, cover and bring to the boil. Lower the heat so the water is simmering gently. Cook for the following times from the moment the water boils: sizes 1 to 3, 10 minutes; sizes 4 to 7, 8 minutes.

To prevent a black ring forming around the egg yolk: when cooked drain off the hot water immediately, crack the eggs to allow the steam to escape and cool rapidly under cold running water.

Coddled Eggs: These are very soft eggs, cooked by steaming in an egg coddler. They are ideal for children and invalids.

Break the egg into a coddler, season lightly if wished and screw or clip the lid in position. Place the coddler in simmering water to come about three quarters of the way up the side. Turn off the heat and leave for the following times: sizes 1 to 3, 8 to 9 minutes; sizes 4 to 7, 6 to 7 minutes.

Baked Eggs: These are traditionally prepared in individual porcelain ramekin or cocotte dishes and usually referred to as eggs *en cocotte*.

Butter the dish and place in a roasting pan containing

about 2.5 cm (1 inch) warm water. Break the egg into the dish and season lightly. Add a knob of butter and cook in a preheated moderate oven, 180°C (350°F), Gas Mark 4, for 8 to 10 minutes or until just set.

Scrambled Eggs: To prepare two servings, break 3 to 4 eggs into a bowl, season to taste with salt and pepper and whisk well with a fork. Melt 25 g (1 oz) butter in a small heavy-based pan over a low heat; don't let it brown. Add the eggs and stir with a wire whisk or wooden spoon until just set enough to hold its shape. Serve immediately on toast. If the eggs are left in the pan even for a short time, they will set into a 'scrambled omelet'!

Fried Eggs: Heat a knob of fat in a frying pan until hot but not smoking. Add the eggs one at a time. They should not sizzle or spit and the white should set slowly. Baste frequently until the yolk is set and serve immediately.

Poached Eggs: This is one of the most difficult methods of preparing eggs. The eggs must be really fresh, the water barely simmering and ideally the pan should be a shallow non-stick frying pan.

Pour water into the pan to a depth of 3.5 cm (1½ inches) and heat until simmering. Break the eggs onto a saucer then slide carefully into the water. Cook for 2 to 3 minutes until just set. If wished, cover the pan or baste the eggs with water during cooking to make the yolk firmer. Remove from the water with a fish slice and drain well before serving on hot buttered toast.

It is not necessary to add salt and vinegar to the water. This was done originally to stop stale eggs from disintegrating, but it has an adverse effect on the flavour and texture of the egg.

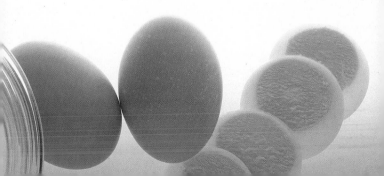

PANCAKES, CRÊPES & FRITTERS

Pancakes and crêpes are made from a similar mixture, though crêpes are often made with buckwheat flour (available in healthfood shops), while pancakes are usually made with plain or wholemeal flour. If using wholemeal flour, stir in a little more liquid before using. If a batter is made several hours before required it will thicken and should be thinned down with more liquid – water will do.

Fritter batter must be very thick in order to coat the food being cooked thoroughly, without running off. Less liquid is used and the egg white is separated and whisked with an extra white, then folded into the batter. Dipping the food in flour first also helps the batter to stick.

QUANTITY GUIDE

To ensure a good batter of the correct consistency, it is best to make up the basic batter quantities given, although many of the recipes only use a proportion. Left-over batter can be stored in a covered container in the refrigerator for up to three days. However, a much better idea is to make up all the batter into various sized pancakes or crêpes and store them cooked (see page 10). Then you will have a ready supply for those recipes using cooked pancakes.

As a general guide, 30 ml (1 fl oz) batter will make one 15 cm (6 inch) pancake or crêpe.

Basic Batters

The method for making these batters is the same (see below). The quantities given are sufficient to make 16 to 20 small pancakes – about 15 cm (6 inches) in diameter.

SWEET PANCAKE BATTER
125 g (4 oz) plain or
*   wholemeal flour*
pinch of salt
2 teaspoons caster sugar
1 egg
300 ml (½ pint) milk
25 g (1 oz) butter, melted
Makes 475 ml (16 fl oz)

SAVOURY PANCAKE BATTER
Omit the sugar. Increase the salt to ¼ teaspoon.

SWEET CRÊPE BATTER
125 g (4 oz) plain, wholemeal
*   or buckwheat flour*
pinch of salt
50 g (2 oz) caster sugar
2 eggs
250 ml (8 fl oz) milk
25 g (1 oz) butter, melted
½ teaspoon vanilla essence
Makes 500 ml (18 fl oz)

SAVOURY CRÊPE BATTER
Omit the sugar and vanilla. Increase salt to ¼ teaspoon. Replace milk with pale ale.

Sift the dry ingredients into a mixing bowl and make a well in the centre. Add the egg(s) and half the liquid. Gradually mix in the flour to make a smooth, thick batter. Stir in the remaining liquid, melted butter and any flavourings. Beat for 2 to 3 minutes. Pour into a jug and use as required.

If using a blender or food processor, place all ingredients, except half the flour, in the goblet and blend for 30 seconds. Add the remaining flour and blend for a further 30 seconds.

TO COOK PANCAKES OR CRÊPES

Very lightly grease an omelet pan or heavy-based frying pan and place over a high heat until really hot. The easiest way to grease the pan is to rub a block of fat very lightly over the surface of the pan between cooking each pancake or crêpe.

Pour in just enough batter to cover the base very thinly, tilting the pan to ensure it is evenly distributed. When the edges are tinged golden brown and bubbles appear on the surface, toss or turn with a palette knife and cook the other side until golden brown. The side that is cooked first will have a lacy golden brown pattern and should become the outside when the pancake or crêpe is rolled or folded.

Turn onto a warmed heatproof plate, cover and place in a preheated cool oven, 150°C (300°F), Gas Mark 2, or over a pan of hot water to keep hot while cooking remaining batter.

TO STORE PANCAKES OR CRÊPES

If cooking for future use, cool the pancakes or crêpes on a wire rack. When cold, stack, separated by rounds of greased greaseproof paper or clingfilm. Pack closely in quantities of 8 to 12 in foil or a polythene bag. Store in a refrigerator for up to five days or in a freezer for up to four months.

TO REHEAT

Thaw frozen pancakes or crêpes, still wrapped, at room temperature for about 2 hours or in a refrigerator overnight. To thaw them quickly, unwrap, separate and leave at room temperature for 30 minutes.

To reheat individually: Place in a lightly greased pan over high heat for about 30 seconds on each side.

To reheat in stacks: Remove the clingfilm or greased paper and wrap in foil. Place in a preheated moderately hot oven, 190°C (375°F), Gas Mark 5, for 20 to 30 minutes.

Pancake and Crêpe Fillings

Pancakes and crêpes can be served hot or cold, sweet or savoury, to make delicious desserts, snacks, starters or main courses. The fillings below are ideal for pancakes or crêpes; most of the omelet fillings on pages 26–7 are also suitable.

Spread the filling over the pancake or crêpe and roll up; alternatively fold in half or into quarters to enclose filling.

HOT SWEET FILLINGS
Flavoured butter – see
  Crêpes Suzette, page 19.
Mincemeat flavoured with
  brandy.
Stewed fruit.
Cottage cheese with raisins
  and sugar.

COLD SWEET FILLINGS
Ice cream.
Mixed dried fruit with
  lemon, sugar and spice.
Fresh fruit and yogurt.
Sliced banana and cream.

HOT SAVOURY FILLINGS
Smoked fish, natural
  yogurt and lemon juice.
Fried chopped chicken
  livers and bacon.
Mixed vegetables in a thick
  cheese sauce.
Roquefort cheese and
  chopped ham.

COLD SAVOURY FILLINGS
Chopped chicken in curried
  mayonnaise.
Scrambled egg and cress
  with mayonnaise.

Alsace Sausage Crêpes

300 ml (½ pint)
savoury crêpe batter
250–350 g (8–12 oz)
smoked pork
sausage, thinly
sliced (see note)
175 g (6 oz) Gruyère
cheese, grated

TO GARNISH:
2 tablespoons
chopped parsley
1 shallot or ½ onion,
finely chopped
1 clove garlic, crushed

Lightly grease a 20 cm (8 inch) omelet pan or heavy-based frying pan and heat until very hot.

Pour in enough batter to make a very thin crêpe, tilting the pan to ensure an even thickness. When the edges begin to brown, cover with the sausage slices and sprinkle with a little cheese. Place under a preheated very hot grill for 20 to 30 seconds until the cheese melts.

Slide the unfolded crêpe onto a warmed heatproof plate and keep hot in a preheated moderate oven, 160°C (325°F), Gas Mark 3, while preparing the remainder.

Mix together the parsley, shallot or onion and garlic and sprinkle over the crêpes to serve.

Serves 6

NOTE: Choose any of the many smoked sausage varieties now available.

Latkes (Potato Pancakes)

500 g (1 lb) potatoes,
    grated into cold
    water
1 onion, grated
2 eggs (size 4),
    lightly beaten
25 g (1 oz) plain
    flour
¼ teaspoon grated
    nutmeg
salt and pepper
butter or dripping for
    frying

Thoroughly drain the potato and mix with the onion. Squeeze well together then drain, if necessary, in a colander, pressing well to remove any excess liquid. Transfer to a mixing bowl and add the remaining ingredients, with salt and pepper to taste. Mix well.

Heat a little fat in a large, heavy-based frying pan or on a hot griddle until sizzling. Drop dessertspoons of the potato mixture onto the hot surface and spread with the back of the spoon until flat. Cook slowly for 4 to 5 minutes, until crisp and golden brown underneath. Turn with a palette knife and cook the other side.

Turn onto a warm heatproof plate; keep hot in a preheated moderately hot oven, 190°C (375°F), Gas Mark 5, while cooking the remainder.

Serve as soon as possible; these pancakes should be eaten crisp.
Makes about 15

Deep-fried Pancake Parcels

4 hard-boiled eggs,
    finely chopped
3–4 tablespoons salad
    cream
1–2 teaspoons curry
    powder
1 carton mustard and
    cress, trimmed and
    chopped
salt
8 × 18 cm (7 inch)
    savoury pancakes
1 egg, well beaten
125 g (4 oz) fresh
    white breadcrumbs
oil for deep-frying

Mix together the eggs, salad cream, curry powder, mustard and cress, and salt to taste. Spread a little of the mixture onto each pancake. Fold two edges in to meet in the centre, then roll up, completely enclosing the filling.

Brush with beaten egg and roll in the breadcrumbs, taking care to seal the opening. Place close together in a frying basket with the sealed opening underneath. Deep-fry in hot oil for 3 to 4 minutes, until crisp and golden brown. Drain well and serve immediately.
Serves 4

Pikelets

2 teaspoons dried
    yeast
1 teaspoon caster
    sugar
250 ml (8 fl oz)
    warm milk
250 g (8 oz) plain
    flour
1 teaspoon salt
2 eggs

Sprinkle the yeast and sugar into the milk and set aside until just beginning to froth. Whisk lightly.

Sift the flour and salt into a mixing bowl and make a well in the centre. Add the eggs and half the milk mixture and, using a wooden spoon, gradually mix to a smooth, thick consistency. Stir in the remaining milk, cover and set aside in a warm place for about 30 minutes.

Meanwhile, heat a griddle or heavy-based frying pan until very hot; grease well.

Stir the batter lightly and pour enough onto the griddle or pan to make a 13–15 cm (5–6 inch) pikelet; the batter will spread and it will look like a thick pancake. When the surface begins to bubble and the edges are tinged golden brown, turn with a palette knife and cook the other side until lightly browned. Keep hot as for pancakes or crêpes.

Spread liberally with butter and serve immediately.
Makes 8 to 10

Cottage Cheese Blintzes

8 × 18 cm (7 inch)
   sweet pancakes
FILLING:
227 g (8 oz) cottage
   or curd cheese
1 egg (size 4), beaten
50 g (2 oz) caster
   sugar
50 g (2 oz) seedless
   raisins, chopped
1/4 teaspoon ground
   cinnamon
TOPPING:
50 g (2 oz) butter
ground cinnamon

Lay the pancakes on a flat surface. Mix the filling ingredients together and spread a little on each pancake. Fold in quarters to make a triangle.

Spread the top of each triangle with a little of the butter and place in an ovenproof dish. Place in a preheated hot oven, 220°C (425°F), Gas Mark 7, for 8 to 10 minutes, until the butter melts and the pancakes are golden and heated through.

Cool slightly, then sprinkle with cinnamon. Serve with whipped cream.
Serves 4 to 6

Scotch Pancakes

15 g (1/2 oz) butter
1 tablespoon golden
   syrup
1 tablespoon milk
175 g (6 oz) plain
   flour
2 teaspoons baking
   powder
1 teaspoon cream of
   tartar
25 g (1 oz) caster
   sugar
pinch of salt
1 egg (size 1 or 2)
150 ml (1/4 pint) milk

Place the butter, syrup and 1 table-spoon milk in a small pan. Heat gently until melted; leave to cool.

Sift the dry ingredients together into a mixing bowl and make a well in the centre. Add the egg, melted ingredients and half the milk. Using a wooden spoon, gradually mix to a smooth, very thick batter. Stir in the remaining milk and beat for 1 to 2 minutes; the batter should have a very thick coating consistency. Allow to stand for 10 to 15 minutes.

Heat a griddle or heavy-based frying pan over a moderate heat and grease lightly. Drop tablespoons of the batter onto the griddle or pan and cook until the surface is covered with small bursting bubbles. Turn with a palette knife and cook the other side until golden brown.

Keep the pancakes warm and moist in a clean folded tea-towel while cooking the remainder. Serve as soon as possible with butter, syrup or jam.
Makes 16 to 18
NOTE: Any left over are delicious fried with bacon and egg for breakfast.

Crêpe Melba

*4 × 18 cm (7 inch)
cold sweet crêpes*
*4 portions vanilla ice
cream*
*1 × 411 g (14½ oz)
can sliced peaches,
drained*
*2–3 tablespoons
raspberry jam*
*1 tablespoon chopped
nuts (optional)*

Lay the crêpes on a flat surface and
place a portion of ice cream in the
centre of each. Quickly fold over the
edges of the crêpe, enclosing the ice
cream, and place on individual
serving dishes.

Top with the peaches, warmed and
sieved jam and nuts, if using. Serve
immediately.

Serves 4

Breton Crêpes

125 g (4 oz)
buckwheat flour
pinch of salt
2 eggs
150 ml (¼ pint) pale
ale
7 tablespoons water
2 teaspoons corn oil
1 tablespoon brandy
caster sugar for
sprinkling

Prepare the batter as described on page 9 and cook the crêpes in an 18 cm (7 inch) pan as described on page 10.

As the crêpes are cooked, sprinkle lightly with caster sugar and keep hot, as described.

Serve with butter, jam or honey.
Makes 14 to 16

Normandy Apple Crêpes

8 × 13 cm (5 inch)
sweet crêpes
4 cooking apples,
peeled and cut into
thin wedges
75–125 g (3–4 oz)
butter
125 g (4 oz) soft light
brown sugar
ground cinnamon for
sprinkling

Lay the crêpes flat on 2 baking sheets. Arrange the apple wedges in a circle on top, leaving a border of about 1 cm (½ inch). Dot with the butter and sprinkle liberally with the sugar and cinnamon to taste.

Place in a preheated moderate oven, 180°C (350°F), Gas Mark 4, for about 30 minutes, until the apples are just soft but hold their shape. Serve hot.
Serves 4 or 8

Crêpes Suzette

BATTER:
125 g (4 oz) plain flour
pinch of salt
25 g (1 oz) caster sugar
2 eggs
7 tablespoons milk
150 ml (¼ pint) pale ale

ORANGE BUTTER FILLING:
50 g (2 oz) butter
50 g (2 oz) caster sugar
1 tablespoon Curaçao
grated rind of 1 orange

TOPPING:
2 tablespoons Curaçao
juice and grated rind of 1 orange

Prepare the batter as described on page 9. Cook in an 18 cm (7 inch) pan as described on page 10, making 14 to 16 crêpes. Keep warm as described.

To prepare the filling, beat together the butter and sugar until soft and creamy. Gradually beat in the Curaçao and grated rind.

Spread a little orange butter on each crêpe and fold into quarters. Place in a shallow ovenproof serving dish and reheat in a preheated hot oven, 230°C (450°F), Gas Mark 8, for 4 to 5 minutes.

Meanwhile, prepare the topping. Pour the Curaçao and orange juice into a small pan and heat until simmering. Pour over the crêpes and sprinkle with the grated rind. Serve immediately.

Serves 4 to 6

NOTE: To flambé crêpes, heat the Curaçao with 1 tablespoon orange juice in a small pan until simmering. Ignite and pour over the crêpes.

Basic Fritter Batter

125 g (4 oz) plain
  flour
pinch of salt
150 ml (¼ pint) milk
1 egg yolk
25 g (1 oz) butter,
  melted
2 egg whites, stiffly
  beaten

Sift the flour and salt into a mixing bowl and make a well in the centre. Add half the milk and the egg yolk and, using a wooden spoon, gradually mix in the flour. When the mixture becomes very stiff, gradually add the remaining milk, beating well between each addition, to make a very thick batter.

Stir in the melted butter and fold in the egg whites.

Makes about 300 ml (½ pint) batter

Corn Fritters

2 eggs (size 1 or 2),
  separated
15 g (½ oz) plain
  flour
1 × 326 g (11½ oz)
  can sweetcorn,
  drained
salt and pepper
25 g (1 oz) butter,
  margarine or
  dripping for frying

Whisk the egg whites until stiff. Mix together the egg yolks, flour and sweetcorn. Season with salt and pepper to taste and fold in the egg whites.

Heat the fat in a large heavy-based frying pan. When the fat sizzles, drop in tablespoons of the corn batter. Fry until set and lightly browned underneath. Turn with a palette knife and fry the other side until golden. Drain and serve immediately.

Makes 12 to 14

Deep-fried Onion Rings

2 large onions, cut into
  5 mm (¼ inch)
  thick slices
300 ml (½ pint)
  fritter batter
oil for deep-frying

Separate the onion slices into rings; discard the small inside rings.

Drop the onion rings a few at a time into the batter and lift out with a skewer.

Heat the oil in a deep-fryer until a cube of bread turns golden and rises to the surface immediately it is dropped in the pan. Deep-fry the onion rings for 2 to 3 minutes, until crisp and golden brown.

Drain thoroughly and keep hot as for Potato Fritters (opposite) while cooking the remaining rings.

Serves 4 to 6

Potato Fritters

3 medium potatoes
300 ml (½ pint)
fritter batter
oil for deep-frying

Cut each potato lengthways into 6 slices, 3–5 mm (⅛–¼ inch) thick. Spear each slice onto a fork and dip in the batter to coat thoroughly.

Heat the oil in a deep-fryer until a cube of bread turns golden and rises to the surface immediately it is dropped in the pan. Deep-fry a few fritters at a time for about 5 minutes, until crisp and golden. Drain thoroughly and place in a warmed heatproof serving dish. Keep hot in a preheated hot oven, 220°C (425°F), Gas Mark 7, while cooking the remainder. Serve hot.

Makes 16 to 18

VARIATION: Grate or finely chop the potato and stir into the batter. Cook as for Apple and Sultana Fritters (see page 22), for 3 to 4 minutes.

Apple and Sultana Fritters

4 dessert apples,
  peeled, cored and
  finely chopped or
  grated
juice of ½ lemon
2 teaspoons caster
  sugar
25 g (1 oz) sultanas
300 ml (½ pint)
  fritter batter
oil for deep-frying, or
  butter for shallow-
  frying
caster sugar and
  cinnamon to serve

Mix together the apple, lemon juice, sugar and sultanas; fold into the batter.

If deep-frying, heat the oil in a deep-fryer and test as for Potato Fritters (page 21). Drop dessert-spoonfuls of the mixture into the oil and fry for 2 to 3 minutes until crisp and golden brown. If shallow-frying, melt the butter in a pan and fry for 4 to 5 minutes on each side.

Drain well and keep hot (as for Potato Fritters) while cooking the remaining mixture. Sprinkle with sugar and cinnamon and serve hot.

Serves 4

VARIATIONS: Replace the apple with chopped banana or pineapple.

Custard Cream Fritters

50 g (2 oz) custard
  powder
284 ml (½ pint)
  single cream or
  milk
2 egg yolks
25 g (1 oz) caster
  sugar
½ teaspoon vanilla
  essence, or 2–3
  teaspoons dark rum
  or orange liqueur
1 egg white

Put the custard powder in a heavy-based pan and blend with a little of the cream or milk to make a thin paste. Stir in the remaining cream or milk. Bring slowly to the boil, stirring, until very thick. Remove from the heat.

Beat in the egg yolks and the sugar. Continue beating until the mixture is cool. Beat in the flavouring and pour into a shallow 15 cm (6 inch) round dish. Set aside until cold and very stiff.

50 g (2 oz) very fine
  fresh white
  breadcrumbs
50 g (2 oz) butter

Brush with the egg white and sprinkle with the breadcrumbs until well coated, pressing on gently.

Melt the butter in an 18 cm (7 inch) heavy-based frying pan over a fairly high heat: the butter must be really hot and frothy but not brown. Fry for about 2 minutes on each side until crisp and golden.

Drain well and cut the mixture into 6 pieces. Serve warm with melted apricot jam or honey.

Makes 6

OMELETS

There are basically two types of omelet: the traditional French plain omelet which is usually savoury and served loosely rolled, and the soufflé omelet which can be savoury but is often served as a dessert, folded or 'open faced'.

The Spanish omelet is a French plain omelet with a substantial savoury filling, served 'open faced' or in wedges.

The best omelet pans are heavy-based for even heat distribution and are often, though not necessarily, non-stick. A 2 to 3-egg mixture needs a 15 cm (6 inch) pan and will serve one person.

Preheat the pan over a moderate heat for 1 to 2 minutes, then add the butter. If the temperature is correct, the butter will melt and sizzle quickly but not brown; if it doesn't, heat until the butter sizzles. Add the eggs and cook until set (see opposite). A French plain omelet should be cooked and served in about 60 seconds.

A soufflé or filled omelet will take longer; the exact time depends on the type and amount of filling.

Plain Omelet

2 or 3 eggs
salt and pepper
15 g (½ oz) butter

Break the eggs into a bowl, add salt and pepper to taste and beat lightly with a fork until well mixed but not frothy. Melt the butter in a preheated pan until sizzling. Add the eggs immediately. As the edge begins to set, draw the mixture towards the centre with a fork and, at the same time, tilt the pan slightly allowing the uncooked egg to run from the centre onto the hot base of the pan to set quickly.

When the omelet is lightly browned underneath but still soft and creamy on top, tilt the pan and fold over about one third of the omelet towards the centre, using a fork or palette knife. Fold over again, making a very loose roll, and turn onto a warmed serving plate. Serve immediately.
Serves 1

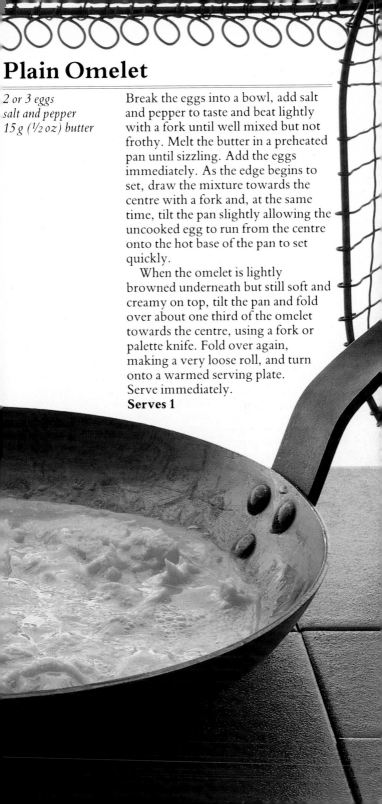

Fillings

Plain omelets can be filled with a variety of savoury mixtures.
Spread the filling over the omelet as it begins to set, before
folding. These quantities are sufficient for one omelet:

ENGLISH–STYLE

25 g (1 oz) smoked
  streaky bacon
25 g (1 oz) mushrooms
15 g (½ oz) butter

Chop the bacon and mushrooms.
Melt the butter in a pan, add the bacon
and mushrooms and fry lightly.
Keep hot while preparing the omelet.

SWISS–STYLE

2 tablespoons single
  cream
25 g (1 oz) Gruyère
  cheese, grated
1 teaspoon chopped
  chives
salt and pepper

Pour the cream over the omelet then
sprinkle with the cheese, chives, and
salt and pepper to taste.

ITALIAN–STYLE

15 g (½ oz) butter
1 tablespoon chopped
  onion
4 black olives, stoned
1 × 227 g (8 oz) can
  tomatoes
¼ teaspoon dried
  oregano
salt and pepper

Melt the butter in a pan, add the onion and fry until soft. Chop the olives and add to the pan with the tomatoes and their juice, oregano, and salt and pepper to taste. Simmer for 10 to 15 minutes until most of the liquid has evaporated and a thick purée forms.

BELGIAN–STYLE

1 shallot or small
  onion, finely
  chopped
1 clove garlic, crushed
1 tablespoon finely
  chopped parsley
salt and pepper

Mix together all the ingredients, seasoning well with salt and pepper.

Soufflé Omelet

Soufflé omelets are usually filled with a sweet mixture and served as a dessert. The various fillings suggested are given in quantities for one omelet.

2 eggs, separated
2 teaspoons cold water
2 teaspoons caster sugar
¼ teaspoon vanilla essence
15 g (½ oz) butter
icing sugar for sprinkling

Whisk together the egg yolks, water, sugar and vanilla essence until pale and creamy. Whisk the egg whites until just stiff enough to stand in peaks, then gently fold both mixtures together with a metal spoon.

Melt the butter in a preheated pan until just beginning to sizzle. Add the egg mixture and spread evenly. Cook gently for about 2 minutes until set around the edge, then place under a preheated moderately hot grill for 1 to 2 minutes until the surface feels firm to the touch and looks puffy.

Alternatively, place in a preheated moderately hot oven, 200°C (400°F), Gas Mark 6, for 3 to 4 minutes.

Fold the omelet in half and turn onto a warmed plate. Sprinkle with icing sugar and serve immediately.

Serves 1

NOTE: For a richer version, fill with strawberry conserve and top with 2–3 tablespoons thick cream.

SWISS-STYLE FILLING

50 g (2 oz) plain
  chocolate
2 tablespoons black
  cherry conserve,
  warmed
icing sugar for
  sprinkling

Grate the chocolate coarsely or make curls with a potato peeler. Slide the unfolded omelet onto a warmed serving plate. Spread with the conserve and fold in half. Top with the chocolate and sprinkle lightly with icing sugar. Serve immediately.

ITALIAN-STYLE FILLING

2 scoops Neapolitan
  ice cream
2 teaspoons crunch-
  nut topping

Slide the unfolded omelet onto a serving plate, top with the ice cream, sprinkle with the nuts and serve immediately.

FRENCH-STYLE FILLING

2 tablespoons orange
  marmalade,
  warmed
2 tablespoons
  Cointreau or
  Grand Marnier
grated rind of
  1 orange

While the omelet is still in the pan, spread with a little of the marmalade. Fold in half and turn onto a warmed serving plate. Stir the liqueur into the remaining marmalade, warm gently and pour over the omelet. Sprinkle with the orange rind and serve immediately.

Piperade

50 g (2 oz) butter
1 onion, chopped
1 clove garlic, crushed
1 green pepper,
    cored, seeded and
    thinly sliced
1 red pepper, cored,
    seeded and thinly
    sliced
3 tomatoes, skinned,
    seeded and chopped
salt and pepper
4 eggs
1 teaspoon chopped
    parsley
4–6 grilled back
    bacon rashers

Melt half the butter in a saucepan, add the garlic and vegetables and sauté gently until soft but not browned. Season with salt and pepper to taste.

Lightly whisk the eggs with the parsley. Heat remaining butter in a preheated 20 cm (8 inch) omelet pan over a high heat until sizzling. Pour in the eggs and cook until just beginning to set, then quickly stir in the vegetable mixture. Lower heat and continue cooking, without stirring, until just set. Slide unfolded onto a warmed serving dish. Top with the bacon and serve immediately.
Serves 2

Omelet Lorraine

3 eggs
salt and pepper
50 g (2 oz) cooked
    ham, shredded
50 g (2 oz) Gruyère
    cheese, grated
15 g (1/2 oz) butter
watercress to garnish

Lightly whisk the eggs with salt and pepper to taste and stir in half the ham and cheese.

Melt the butter in a preheated 20 cm (8 inch) omelet pan until sizzling. Pour in the eggs and cook until beginning to set but still soft in the centre.

Sprinkle over the remaining ham and cheese and fold the omelet in half. Turn onto a warmed serving dish and serve, garnished with watercress.
Serves 1 to 2

Bornholm Herring Omelet

4 eggs
4 tablespoons milk
salt and pepper
25 g (1 oz) butter
1 onion, chopped
4 tomatoes, sliced
2 smoked herring,
    filleted and flaked
1 tablespoon chopped
    chives

Whisk the eggs lightly with the milk and a little salt and pepper.

Melt the butter in a preheated 20 cm (8 inch) omelet pan until sizzling. Add the egg mixture and cook gently. While the top is still soft, cover with the onion, tomatoes and herring. When just set, sprinkle with the chives. Slide unfolded onto a warmed serving plate and serve.
Serves 2

Normandy Omelet

4 mussels, scrubbed
    clean (optional)
50 g (2 oz) peeled
    prawns
3 tablespoons dry
    white wine
1 small bay leaf
1 parsley sprig
3 tablespoons double
    cream
salt and pepper
25 g (1 oz) butter
3 eggs, lightly beaten
TO GARNISH:
3–4 cooked whole
    prawns
parsley sprig

Place the mussels, if using, in a small pan, cover with cold water and bring to the boil. Simmer for about 5 minutes, until the shells open; discard any that do not. Remove from the pan, cool slightly then chop.

Place the mussels and prawns in a small pan. Add the wine, bay leaf and parsley and simmer, uncovered, until all the excess liquid has evaporated. Remove the bay leaf and parsley and stir in the cream. Season with salt and pepper to taste.

Melt the butter in a preheated 20 cm (8 inch) omelet pan until sizzling. Add the eggs and cook until just beginning to set. Spoon the prepared fish mixture over the omelet and fold in half. Turn onto a warmed serving dish, garnish with the prawns and parsley. Serve immediately.
Serves 1 to 2

Omelet Arnold Bennett

50 g (2 oz) butter
4 tablespoons single
    cream
125 g (4 oz) smoked
    haddock, cooked
    and flaked
salt and pepper
3 eggs, separated
15 g (½ oz) grated
    Parmesan cheese
a little chopped
    parsley to garnish

Melt half the butter in a small saucepan. Remove from the heat and stir in half the cream and the fish. Season with salt and pepper to taste.

Stir the egg yolks into the fish mixture. Whisk the egg whites until just stiff enough to form peaks. Fold in the fish mixture and half the cheese.

Melt the remaining butter in a preheated 20 cm (8 inch) omelet pan. Add the fish mixture and spread evenly in the pan. Cook fairly quickly until just beginning to set.

Sprinkle with the remaining cheese and place under a very hot grill until the cheese is lightly browned. Slide the unfolded omelet onto a warmed serving dish. Pour over the remaining cream, sprinkle with parsley and serve immediately.
Serves 1 to 2

Spanish Omelet

75 g (3 oz) butter
1 onion, chopped
1 small red pepper,
    cored, seeded and
    shredded
1 small green pepper,
    cored, seeded and
    shredded
1 potato, diced
1 carrot, diced
1 courgette, sliced
1–2 cloves garlic,
    crushed
salt and pepper
4 eggs, lightly beaten

Melt 50 g (2 oz) of the butter in a pan, add the vegetables and garlic, cover with a tight-fitting lid and cook for about 10 minutes, until tender, shaking the pan frequently. Season well with salt and pepper.

Melt the remaining butter in a preheated 25 cm (10 inch) omelet pan or frying pan until sizzling. Add the cooked vegetables, together with the juices.

Pour over the eggs and shake the pan gently to distribute the vegetables evenly. Lower the heat and cook until the omelet is set. Slide unfolded onto a warmed serving plate and serve immediately.

Serves 2

33

SOUFFLÉS & MOUSSES

Soufflés may be hot or cold, sweet or savoury, but they should always be light and fluffy, with an open honeycomb texture. A mousse has a closer, more velvety texture and is always served cold.

A soufflé is made in the traditional straight-sided soufflé dish and is never turned out. A mousse can be made in a variety of serving dishes, but is often moulded and turned out for serving. Always use the dish size recommended, as the capacity will affect setting and baking times.

There is no secret to the success of a soufflé or mousse, but the following guidelines may help:

To dissolve gelatine: place in a small bowl, add the cold water and leave for a few minutes until it swells and forms a stiff paste. Stand the bowl over a pan of hot water and stir until the gelatine dissolves to a completely clear liquid. Any cloudiness means it has not completely dissolved and will not set the mixture. Never boil the gelatine – it will become stringy and useless.

Gelatine is available in 11 g (0.4 oz) envelopes. Where a recipe specifies one envelope, this is the size to use.

COLD SOUFFLÉS

A cold soufflé should stand at least 2.5 cm (1 inch) above the top of the dish. Cut a band of double greaseproof paper long enough to go around the outside of the dish and wide enough to stand about 5 cm (2 inches) above the rim. Secure with string or an elastic band and hold the paper together at the top with paper clips if necessary.

When the soufflé has set, remove the string or elastic band and paper clips, if used. Hold a palette knife against the side of the soufflé and carefully peel off the paper while sliding the knife around the soufflé.

HOT SOUFFLÉS

A paper band is not necessary. A baked soufflé should rise well, be golden brown and firm on top, but soft in the centre. Too hot an oven will set the top of the mixture before it can rise; too cool an oven will cause the soufflé to collapse when the oven door is opened. Always cook at the temperature given and, unless otherwise stated, use the centre shelf. A hot soufflé must be served immediately.

MOUSSES

For mousses which are to be turned out, rinse the mould with cold water before filling.

When making a decorative moulded mousse, the garnish is often set in gelatine first in the base of the mould. Take care not to disturb this layer when pouring in the mousse mixture: pour it in very slowly.

To turn out a moulded mousse, loosen the edge of the mould with the fingertips. Dip into a bowl of hand-hot water until the water level reaches the top of the mould. If the mould is metal, take it out immediately; if china, count slowly to ten before doing so. Place a plate over the mould, invert and shake once or twice to release the mousse.

Cheese and Herb Soufflé

40 g (1½ oz) butter
40 g (1½ oz) plain
    flour
284 ml (½ pint) half
    cream or milk
3 eggs (size 1),
    separated
1 × 150 g (5 oz)
    packet full fat soft
    cheese with garlic
    and herbs,
    crumbled
salt and pepper

Melt the butter in a pan, add the flour and cook, stirring, for 1 minute. Remove from the heat and gradually stir in the cream or milk, mixing well between each addition. Bring to the boil, stirring until thickened.

Remove from the heat and beat in the egg yolks, one at a time. Add the cheese and stir until melted. Season with a little salt and pepper. Leave to cool.

Whisk the egg whites until just stiff enough to stand in peaks. Mix about 2 tablespoons into the cheese mixture, making it soft and 'slack'. Carefully fold the egg whites and cheese mixture together with a metal spoon.

Turn into a buttered 1.2 litre (2 pint) soufflé dish, placed on a baking sheet. Bake immediately in a preheated moderately hot oven, 190°C (375°F), Gas Mark 5, for 35 to 40 minutes, until well risen and golden brown. Serve immediately.
Serves 3 to 4

Layered Cheese and Tomato Soufflé

25 g (1 oz) butter
1 clove garlic, crushed
1 small onion,
    chopped
350 g (12 oz)
    tomatoes, skinned
    and chopped
2 teaspoons dried
    oregano
6–8 black olives,
    stoned and chopped
salt and pepper
Cheese and herb
    soufflé mixture
    (see recipe)

Melt the butter in a pan, add the garlic, onion and tomatoes and fry lightly for 3 to 4 minutes. Add the oregano and olives, and salt and pepper to taste. Allow to cool.

Prepare the soufflé mixture (see above). Spread the tomato mixture in a buttered 1.5 litre (2½ pint) soufflé dish placed on a baking sheet and cover with the soufflé mixture. Bake immediately in a preheated moderately hot oven, 190°C (375°F), Gas Mark 5, for 35 to 40 minutes, until well risen and golden brown. Serve immediately.
Serves 4

Peppered Mackerel Soufflé

40 g (1½ oz) butter
40 g (1½ oz) plain
   flour
300 ml (½ pint) milk
3 eggs (size 1),
   separated
142 ml (5 fl oz)
   soured cream
300–350 g
   (10–12 oz)
   peppered smoked
   mackerel, flaked
1 tablespoon lemon
   juice
1 tablespoon chopped
   parsley

Melt the butter in a pan, add the flour and cook, stirring, for 1 minute. Remove from the heat and gradually stir in the milk, mixing well between each addition. Bring to the boil, stirring, until thickened.

Remove from the heat and beat in the egg yolks, one at a time, then the soured cream. Stir in the mackerel, lemon juice and parsley. Leave to cool.

Whisk the egg whites until stiff. Stir about 2 tablespoons into the fish mixture, to make it soft. Carefully fold the egg whites into the fish mixture, using a metal spoon.

Turn into a buttered 1.2 litre (2 pint) soufflé dish placed on a baking sheet. Bake immediately in a preheated moderately hot oven, 190°C (375°F), Gas Mark 5, for 45 to 50 minutes, until well risen and golden brown. Serve immediately.
Serves 4

Salmon Mousse

300 ml (½ pint) milk
3 white peppercorns
1 bay leaf
1 blade mace
1 onion, stuck with
* 2 cloves*
1 small carrot
1 envelope gelatine,
* dissolved in*
* 2 tablespoons water*
150 ml (¼ pint) dry
* white wine*
¼ cucumber, sliced
40 g (1½ oz) butter
25 g (1 oz) plain
* flour*
2 eggs, separated
2 × 99 g (3½ oz)
* cans red salmon,*
* drained*
salt and pepper
2–3 tablespoons
* single cream*
TO GARNISH:
lemon twist
gherkin slices
olive slices

Put the milk in a pan with the peppercorns, bay leaf, mace, onion and carrot and leave to infuse over very low heat for 15 minutes.

Add the dissolved gelatine to the wine. Pour a little onto the base of a 900 ml (1½ pint) mould and leave to set. Arrange cucumber slices on top, cover with a little wine and leave to set; keep remaining wine warm to prevent setting.

Strain the milk into a pan and add the butter and flour. Bring to the boil, whisking constantly. Remove from the heat, cool slightly and beat in the egg yolks, one at a time. Add the salmon, and salt and pepper to taste.

Work the mixture in an electric blender or food processor until smooth. Stir in the remaining wine and the cream. Whisk the egg whites until stiff and fold into the mixture. Turn into the mould and chill for 2 hours or until set. Turn out and serve garnished with lemon, gherkin and olive slices.

Serves 6

Tarragon Chicken Mousse

3 eggs, separated
15 g (½ oz) cornflour
150 ml (¼ pint)
 chicken stock
142 ml (5 fl oz)
 soured cream
1 tablespoon tarragon
 vinegar
1 tablespoon chopped
 fresh or 2 teaspoons
 dried tarragon
1 envelope gelatine,
 dissolved in
 2 tablespoons
 boiling water
350 g (12 oz) cooked
 chicken, minced
salt and pepper
TO GARNISH:
lemon slices
tarragon leaves or
 watercress sprigs

Blend the egg yolks with the
cornflour and stock in a pan. Place
over a moderate heat and stir
constantly until thickened; *do not boil*.

Remove from the heat, cool
slightly, then stir in the soured cream,
vinegar, tarragon, dissolved gelatine
and chicken. Season well with salt
and pepper. Leave until the mixture is
just beginning to set, stirring
occasionally. Whisk the egg whites
until just stiff and fold in carefully but
thoroughly with a metal spoon.

Turn into a 1.2 litre (2 pint) soufflé
dish or ring mould and refrigerate for
about 2 hours or until set.

Turn out onto a serving dish and
garnish with lemon slices and
tarragon or watercress.
Serves 4 to 6

Stilton Mousse

1 envelope gelatine
150 ml (¼ pint)
   chicken stock
few cucumber slices
50 g (2 oz) butter
2 onions, chopped
2 cloves garlic, crushed
25 g (1 oz) cornflour
350 ml (12 fl oz)
   milk
1 bay leaf
300 g (10 oz) blue
   Stilton cheese,
   crumbled
2 egg yolks
2–3 tablespoons
   single cream
1 tablespoon chopped
   parsley
salt and pepper
TO GARNISH:
cucumber slices
parsley sprigs or
   rosemary

Dissolve the gelatine in the chicken stock; cool slightly. Pour a little into the base of a 1.2 litre (2 pint) mould, arrange a few cucumber slices in the stock and leave to set. Keep remaining stock warm so it doesn't set.

Melt the butter in a pan, add the onions and garlic and sauté until soft but not browned. Remove from the heat, stir in the cornflour, then gradually stir in the milk. Add the bay leaf and cheese and bring to the boil, stirring.

Cool slightly, discard bay leaf and beat in the egg yolks, one at a time. Sieve or work in an electric blender or food processor until smooth.

Stir in the cream, remaining stock, parsley, and salt and pepper to taste. Pour slowly into the prepared mould and chill overnight, or until set.

Turn out onto a serving dish and garnish with cucumber and herbs.
Serves 6 to 8

Coffee and Walnut Mousse

1 tablespoon coffee
  granules
2 tablespoons boiling
  water
4 egg yolks
50 g (2 oz) soft light
  brown sugar
50 g (2 oz) walnuts,
  finely ground
142 ml (5 fl oz)
  whipping cream,
  whipped
TO DECORATE:
4 teaspoons Tia
  Maria (optional)
4 walnut halves

Blend the coffee granules with the boiling water in a mixing bowl. Add the egg yolks, sugar and walnuts and place the bowl over a pan of simmering water. Whisk until creamy and thick enough to leave a trail.

Remove from the pan and continue whisking until the mixture is cold and thick enough to hold its shape. Fold in the cream.

Spoon into individual serving dishes and top each with a teaspoonful of Tia Maria, if using, and half a walnut. Serve chilled.
Serves 4

Damson Meringue Mousse

1 × 397 g (14 oz)
  can damsons
1 envelope gelatine,
  dissolved in
  2 tablespoons
  water
1 × 170 g (6 oz) can
  evaporated milk
3 teaspoons lemon
  juice
2 egg whites
50 g (2 oz) caster
  sugar
TO DECORATE:
3–4 tablespoons
  double cream,
  whipped
pistachio nuts or
  toasted slivered
  almonds

Drain the juice from the damsons and make up to 200 ml (⅓ pint) with warm water. Stir in the dissolved gelatine. Sieve the damsons to remove the stones and stir the purée into the fruit juice. Chill until beginning to thicken.

Pour the evaporated milk into a large mixing bowl. Add the lemon juice and whisk until thick and creamy. Stir in the thickened fruit juice mixture and leave until just beginning to set.

Whisk the egg whites until stiff, then gradually whisk in the sugar to make a soft meringue. Carefully fold into the fruit mixture.

Turn into a dampened 1.2 litre (2 pint) mould or individual dishes and chill until set, preferably overnight.

Turn out onto a serving plate and decorate with piped cream and nuts.
Serves 6

Chocolate and Peppermint Mousse

284 ml (½ pint)
    whipping cream,
    well chilled
½ teaspoon
    peppermint essence
¼ teaspoon green
    food colouring
    (optional)
2 egg whites
1 tablespoon icing or
    caster sugar
24 chocolate
    peppermint sticks,
    chopped

Pour the cream into a bowl and add the essence, colouring if using, egg whites and sugar. Whisk until stiff enough to stand in peaks and at least doubled in volume. Fold in the chopped chocolate peppermint sticks.

Spoon into individual freezerproof serving dishes and place in a freezer for about 2 hours, until well chilled and just on the point of freezing. Serve immediately.
Serves 4 to 6

Chocolate Cinnamon Soufflé

1 tablespoon cocoa
   powder
2 tablespoons boiling
   water
4 eggs, separated
125 g (4 oz) caster
   sugar
1½ teaspoons ground
   cinnamon
1 envelope gelatine,
   dissolved in
   2 tablespoons water
142 ml (5 fl oz)
   whipping cream,
   half whipped
TO DECORATE:
150 g (6 oz) plain
   chocolate

Blend the cocoa with the boiling water to a smooth paste; cool.

Put the egg yolks, sugar, cinnamon and cocoa paste in a mixing bowl over a pan of simmering water. Whisk until creamy and thick enough to leave a trail. Remove from the heat and whisk until cool. Whisk the egg whites until stiff.

Pour the dissolved gelatine into the chocolate mixture in a slow continuous stream, stirring gently. Carefully fold in the half-whipped cream and whisked egg whites.

Turn into a prepared 900 ml (1½ pint) cold soufflé dish and chill for 2 hours or until set. Meanwhile, shave half the chocolate into curls, using a potato peeler; finely grate the remainder.

Carefully peel off the paper band from the soufflé and press the grated chocolate around the sides. Arrange the chocolate curls on top.
Serves 4 to 6

Crystallized Ginger Soufflé

50-75 g (2–3 oz)
  crystallized ginger,
  minced or finely
  chopped
2 tablespoons boiling
  water
4 eggs, separated
25 g (1 oz) caster
  sugar
1 envelope gelatine,
  dissolved in
  2 tablespoons water
142 ml (5 fl oz)
  whipping cream,
  half whipped
TO DECORATE:
50–75 g (2–3 oz)
  chopped nuts
few pieces
  crystallized ginger,
  chopped

Put the ginger in a mixing bowl and
sprinkle on the boiling water. Add
the egg yolks and sugar and place the
bowl over a pan of simmering water.
Whisk until creamy and thick enough
to leave a trail. Remove from pan and
whisk until cool. Whisk the egg
whites until stiff.

Pour the dissolved gelatine into the
ginger mixture in a slow continuous
stream, stirring gently.

Carefully fold in the half-whipped
cream, reserving 2 tablespoons for
decoration, and the whisked egg
whites. Turn into a prepared 900 ml
(1½ pint) cold soufflé dish and chill
for 2 hours or until set.

Peel off the paper band and press
the nuts around the side. Decorate
with the reserved cream and ginger.
Serves 4 to 6

Pineapple Soufflé: Replace the
ginger with 75–125 g (3–4 oz)
crystallized pineapple.

Baked Chocolate Soufflé

25 g (1 oz) cocoa
   powder
40 g (1½ oz)
   cornflour
300 ml (½ pint) milk
50 g (2 oz) caster
   sugar
50 g (2 oz) butter
4 eggs, separated
1 teaspoon vanilla
   essence
25 g (1 oz) icing
   sugar, sifted, to
   serve

Blend the cocoa and cornflour with a little of the milk in a pan. Add the remaining milk, the sugar and butter and cook, stirring, until thickened. Cool slightly, then beat in the egg yolks, one at a time, and vanilla.

Whisk the egg whites until stiff. Fold about 2 tablespoons into the chocolate mixture, making it soft, then carefully fold in the remainder.

Turn into an oiled 1.2 litre (2 pint) soufflé dish and bake immediately in a preheated moderate oven, 180°C (350°F), Gas Mark 4, for 35 to 40 minutes, until risen and firm on top.

Sprinkle with icing sugar and serve immediately.
Serves 4

Milanaise Soufflé

3 eggs, separated
75 g (3 oz) caster
   sugar
grated rind and juice
   of 2 lemons
1 envelope gelatine,
   dissolved in 2
   tablespoons water
142 ml (5 fl oz)
   whipping cream,
   half whipped
TO DECORATE:
50–75 g (2–3 oz)
   chopped nuts
crystallized lemon
   slices (optional)

Place the egg yolks, sugar, lemon rind and juice in a bowl over a pan of simmering water and whisk until thick enough to leave a trail. Remove from the pan and whisk until cool. Whisk egg whites until stiff.

Pour the dissolved gelatine into the lemon mixture in a slow continuous stream, stirring gently. Carefully fold in the cream, reserving 2 tablespoons for decoration, and the whisked egg whites. Turn into a prepared 900 ml (1½ pint) cold soufflé dish and chill for 2 hours or until set.

Peel off the paper and press nuts around side. Decorate with reserved cream and lemon slices, if wished.
Serves 4 to 6

Lime or Orange Soufflé: Replace the lemons with the grated rind and juice of 3 limes, or 2 oranges.
Coffee Soufflé: Replace the lemons with 2 tablespoons coffee granules dissolved in 2 tablespoons hot water.

Soufflé Rothschild

1 peach or mango,
  diced
1 kiwi fruit, diced
8 strawberries, diced
2 slices fresh or
  canned pineapple,
  diced
1 miniature bottle
  Curaçao
4 eggs, separated
50 g (2 oz) caster
  sugar
25 g (1 oz) icing
  sugar, sifted, to
  serve

Place all the fruits in a shallow dish and pour over the Curaçao. Set aside for about 1 hour, turning the fruit occasionally.

Drain the excess juice from the fruit into a mixing bowl and add the egg yolks and caster sugar. Place over a pan of simmering water and whisk until creamy and thick enough to leave a trail. Remove from the pan and whisk until cool. Whisk the egg whites until stiff and carefully fold both mixtures together.

Place the fruit in a buttered 1.2 litre (2 pint) soufflé dish on a baking sheet. Spoon the soufflé mixture on top of the fruit.

Bake immediately in a preheated moderate oven, 180°C (350°F), Gas Mark 4, for 20 minutes. The soufflé should be well risen, golden brown on top and creamy in the centre.

Dredge with icing sugar and serve immediately.

Serves 4 to 6

NOTE: If preferred, use individual dishes and cook for 10 minutes.

Soufflé Surprise

3 eggs, separated
50 g (2 oz) caster
   sugar
1 tablespoon sweet
   sherry
2 × 227 g (8 oz)
   packets frozen
   blackberries, half
   thawed
1/3 litre (12 oz) block
   vanilla ice cream
15 g (1/2 oz) icing
   sugar, sifted

Lightly butter a 1.5 litre (2½ pint) soufflé dish and place in a shallow dish or pan surrounded by ice cubes. Place in the refrigerator while preparing the soufflé mixture.

Put the egg yolks, sugar and sherry in a mixing bowl over a pan of simmering water and whisk until creamy and thick enough to leave a trail. Remove from the pan and whisk until cool.

Whisk the egg whites until stiff and, using a metal spoon, fold in the yolk mixture. Remove the prepared dish from the refrigerator and immediately put the blackberries in the bottom. Place the ice cream on top and quickly cover with the soufflé mixture.

Sprinkle with the icing sugar and bake immediately on the top shelf of a preheated moderately hot oven, 200°C (400°F), Gas Mark 6, for 8 to 10 minutes, until well risen and golden brown. Serve immediately.
Serves 4 to 6

49

SALADS & COLD SNACKS

American Potato Salad

500 g (1 lb) small
  new potatoes,
  boiled and skinned
125 g (4 oz) piece
  salami
2 celery sticks
1 tablespoon chopped
  chives
1 tablespoon chopped
  parsley
6–8 tablespoons
  mayonnaise
4 hard-boiled eggs
TO GARNISH:
bunch of watercress
paprika

Thinly slice the potatoes, dice the salami and chop the celery. Place in a large bowl with the chives, parsley and mayonnaise.

Cut the eggs in half and remove and sieve the yolks. Add half to the ingredients in the bowl, keep the other half on one side. Chop the whites and add to the bowl.

Turn the ingredients over gently until thoroughly mixed, without breaking the potato.

Serve on a bed of watercress and garnish with the reserved egg yolk and paprika.

Serves 4 to 6

Egg and Corn Salad

3 eggs, lightly
 scrambled (see
 page 7)
1 × 198 g (7 oz) can
 sweetcorn, drained
4 tablespoons sauce
 Indienne (see page
 92), or mayonnaise
8 large slices German
 garlic sausage or
 Bierwurst
1 lettuce, shredded
2–3 leaves red
 cabbage, finely
 shredded
2 tablespoons French
 dressing
watercress to garnish

Mix together the eggs, corn and sauce
Indienne or mayonnaise.

Cut a quarter out of each slice of
sausage and shred it into matchstick-
size strips.

Place the lettuce, red cabbage and
sausage strips in a serving dish.
Spoon over the French dressing and
toss lightly.

Roll the sausage slices into cones,
fill with the egg and corn mixture and
place on the lettuce mixture. Garnish
with watercress.
Serves 4

Salade Niçoise

8 anchovy fillets
3–4 tablespoons milk
125 g (4 oz) small
    French beans
salt
pinch of ground
    nutmeg
½ small cucumber
250 g (8 oz) tomatoes
4 hard-boiled eggs
250 g (8 oz)
    peppered smoked
    mackerel
3–4 tablespoons
    French dressing
TO GARNISH:
8–12 black olives,
    stoned

Soak the anchovy fillets in the milk for 15 to 20 minutes. Drain and discard the milk.

Cook the beans in lightly salted boiling water, with the nutmeg added, until just tender but still firm. Drain, rinse under cold running water and drain again.

Cut the cucumber into sticks about half the size of the beans. Season very lightly with salt.

Cut the tomatoes and eggs into quarters and flake the mackerel.

Arrange all the ingredients in a shallow serving dish. Pour over the French dressing and garnish with the olives.

Serves 4

NOTE: For a traditional French *salade Niçoise*, use tuna in place of mackerel.

Danish Salad

4 hard-boiled eggs
1 green dessert apple
1 red dessert apple
4 pickled Danish
    sweetened herring
    fillets
4 small pickled
    beetroots, diced
2 pickled dill
    cucumbers, sliced
4 small potatoes,
    boiled and diced
142 ml (5 fl oz)
    soured cream or
    natural yogurt
salt and pepper
TO GARNISH:
chopped parsley

Slice the eggs, dice the apples and cut the herrings into small pieces.

Place the egg slices and dill cucumber slices around the edge of a serving dish. Arrange the beetroot in a circle within the egg. Mix the remaining ingredients together, seasoning with salt and pepper to taste, and spoon into the centre of the beetroot ring.

Sprinkle with chopped parsley.

Serves 4 to 6

Veal, Ham and Egg Pie

HOT WATERCRUST
  PASTRY:
*500 g (1 lb) plain
  flour*
1½ teaspoons salt
1 egg + 1 extra yolk
6 tablespoons milk
6 tablespoons water
*125 g (4 oz) lard, cut
  into small pieces*
beaten egg to glaze
FILLING:
*500 g (1 lb) pie veal,
  cut into 1 cm
  (½ inch) cubes*
*250 g (8 oz) gammon
  or lean boiling
  bacon, cut into
  1 cm (½ inch)
  cubes*
*1 tablespoon chopped
  fresh or 2 teaspoons
  dried sage*
*grated rind and juice
  of 1 lemon*
salt and pepper
*4 hard-boiled eggs
  (size 5)*
JELLIED STOCK:
*1 envelope gelatine,
  dissolved in 150 ml
  (¼ pint) stock*

Sift the flour and salt into a bowl and make a well in the centre. Blend the egg and extra yolk with 1 tablespoon milk and pour into the flour. Place the remaining milk, the water and lard in a pan and bring to the boil. Pour immediately into the flour and beat to make a soft dough.

Turn onto a floured surface and knead until smooth. Cover and leave in a warm place for 20 minutes.

Mix the filling ingredients together, except the eggs, adding a little salt and pepper. Roll out two thirds of the pastry to a 30 cm (12 inch) circle. Lift carefully into a well greased raised pie mould, or deep 15 cm (6 inch) loose-bottomed cake tin, and mould to fit the tin.

Press half the filling in the tin, place the eggs on top and cover with the remaining filling. Brush the pastry edges with water. Roll out remaining pastry for the lid and place over the filling. Seal and trim the edges.

Decorate with leaves cut from the trimmings. Make a 5 mm (¼ inch) hole in the centre of the pie and place a little ball of dough on top. Brush with egg. Place on a baking sheet and bake in a preheated moderately hot oven, 200°C (400°F), Gas Mark 6, for 30 minutes. Lower the heat to 160°C (325°F), Gas Mark 3, and cook for 1½ hours.

Remove the pie from the tin and place on the baking sheet. Brush all over with egg and return to the oven for 30 minutes.

Remove the pastry ball from the hole and gradually pour in the liquid jellied stock. Leave to cool, then chill overnight. Serve cold.

Serves 8
NOTE: The veal can be replaced with lean pork if preferred.

Egg Mayonnaise Provençal

6 large lettuce leaves
6 hard-boiled eggs
300 ml (½ pint)
    Aioli (see page 92)
2–3 teaspoons tomato
    purée
TO GARNISH:
1 × 184 g (6½ oz)
    can red peppers,
    drained and sliced
12–18 black olives,
    stoned
few rosemary sprigs

Place the lettuce leaves on individual serving plates. Cut the eggs in half and place, cut side down, on the lettuce.

Mix together the Aioli and tomato purée and spoon over the eggs. Garnish with the peppers, olives and rosemary.
Serves 6

Eggs Indienne: Replace the Aioli with Sauce Indienne (page 92). Replace rosemary with parsley.

Layered Eggs

227 g (8 oz) skimmed
milk soft cheese or
curd cheese
125 g (4 oz) blue
Brie
24 thin slices Danish
salami
8 hard-boiled eggs
(size 1)
24 small thin slices
cucumber
24 small thin slices
tomato
24 large thin slices
radish
2 tablespoons French
dressing
2 teaspoons chopped
parsley
mustard and cress to
garnish

Beat both cheeses together very
thoroughly until soft and smooth.
Spoon into a piping bag fitted with a
large star nozzle.

Place the salami on a serving plate
and pipe a ring of cheese mixture on
each, making a little 'nest'. Cut each
egg halfway through into slices,
using a sharp knife carefully place
slices of cucumber, tomato and radish
between the egg slices. Carefully lift
on to the cheese 'nest' and sprinkle
with a little French dressing and
parsley. Garnish with mustard and
cress.
Serves 8

56

Egg and Anchovy Pâté

2 × 50 g (1¾ oz)
  cans anchovy fillets
6–8 stuffed olives,
  halved
25 g (1 oz) butter
1 onion, chopped
1–2 cloves garlic,
  crushed
25 g (1 oz) plain
  flour
150 ml (¼ pint) milk
150 ml (¼ pint) fish
  or chicken stock
3 eggs, beaten
75 g (3 oz) fresh fine
  brown or white
  breadcrumbs
50 g (2 oz) capers
3 hard-boiled eggs,
  chopped
pepper

Grease a 1 kg (2 lb) loaf tin and line
the base with greaseproof paper.
Arrange 8 anchovy fillets and the
olives on the base. Chop remaining
anchovies and reserve, with the oil.

Melt the butter in a pan, add the
onion and garlic and fry gently for
5 minutes. Stir in the flour, then the
milk and stock a little at a time. Bring
to the boil, stirring until thickened.
Remove from the heat and stir in the
anchovies and oil. Cool slightly then
add remaining ingredients, with
pepper to taste. Leave for 15 minutes,
then spoon into the tin.

Bake in a preheated moderate
oven, 180°C (350°F), Gas Mark 4, for
1 hour or until set. Leave until
completely cold.

Turn out and serve with salad.
Serves 8 to 10

Devilled Eggs

6 hard-boiled eggs
4 tablespoons Aïoli
 (see page 92) or
 mayonnaise
1 teaspoon curry
 powder
1/2 teaspoon made
 English mustard
1/2 teaspoon tomato
 purée
TO GARNISH:
mustard and cress
chopped chives
paprika or cayenne

Cut the eggs in half. Remove and
sieve the yolks into a bowl; keep the
whites on one side. Add the
remaining ingredients and mix well
to a smooth, soft paste. Pipe or spoon
the mixture into the egg whites and
arrange on a serving dish. Garnish
with mustard and cress, chives and a
sprinkling of paprika or cayenne.
Serves 4 to 6
VARIATIONS: To the sieved egg yolks
and Aïoli add any of the following:
50 g (2 oz) minced garlic sausage;
mashed smoked mackerel, sardine or
tuna; grated cheese; finely chopped
red and green pepper.

Scotch Eggs

500 g (1 lb)
  sausagemeat
salt and pepper
6 hard-boiled eggs
flour for coating
1 egg, beaten
75–125 g (3–4 oz)
  fine fresh white
  breadcrumbs
oil for deep-frying

Divide the sausagemeat into 6 equal portions. On a floured surface, flatten each into a 7.5 cm (3 inch) circle. Season lightly with salt and pepper.

Dust each egg with flour and place on a round of sausagemeat. Mould the sausagemeat around the egg, taking care to seal the join completely. Brush with egg and coat with breadcrumbs.

Heat the oil and deep-fry for 5 to 6 minutes, until golden brown. Drain well and leave until cold.
Serves 6

Cheddar Eggs: Replace the sausagemeat with 750 g (1½ lb) cooked potatoes, mashed with 125 g (4 oz) finely grated Cheddar cheese and a small, finely chopped onion.

Giant Sausage Roll

1 × 215 g (7½ oz)
  packet frozen puff
  pastry, thawed
1–2 teaspoons made
  English mustard
350 g (12 oz)
  sausagemeat
4 hard-boiled eggs
beaten egg to glaze
parsley sprigs to
  garnish

Roll out the pastry on a lightly floured board to an oblong about 30 × 20 cm (12 × 8 inches). Spread the mustard down the centre.

Flatten the sausagemeat into an oblong about 25 × 13 cm (10 × 5 inches) and place along the centre of the pastry. Place the eggs at intervals in the centre of the sausagemeat.

Brush the edges of the pastry with water and bring the two longer sides together in the middle, enclosing the eggs and sausagemeat. Seal both ends well and carefully lift onto a baking sheet, with the join underneath.

Brush with beaten egg and slash at intervals along the top of the roll.

Bake in a preheated moderately hot oven, 200°C (400°F), Gas Mark 6, for 25 to 30 minutes, until well risen and golden brown. Serve hot or cold, garnished with parsley.
Serves 4 to 6

HOT SAVOURY DISHES

Eggs Florentine

1 × 227 g (8 oz)
    packet frozen
    chopped spinach,
    thawed
salt and pepper
4 soft-boiled eggs (see
    page 6)
CHEESE SAUCE:
25 g (1 oz) butter
25 g (1 oz) plain
    flour
300 ml (½ pint) milk
    or half cream
175 g (6 oz)
    Lancashire or
    Cheddar cheese,
    grated

Line a shallow ovenproof dish with the spinach. Season well with salt and pepper. Place the eggs on top.

To make the sauce, melt the butter in a pan and stir in the flour. Gradually stir in the milk or cream and cook, stirring, until thickened. Lower the heat, add two thirds of the cheese and stir until melted, then pour over the eggs. Sprinkle with remaining cheese.

Bake on the top shelf of a preheated moderately hot oven, 200°C (400°F), Gas Mark 6, for 15 to 20 minutes, until golden brown. Serve immediately.
Serves 2 or 4

Eggs Mornay: Omit the spinach and add 25 g (1 oz) fine fresh breadcrumbs to the cheese for sprinkling.

Eggs Flamenca

1 tablespoon oil
50 g (2 oz) butter
2 potatoes, boiled and
    diced
125 g (4 oz) smoked
    pepper sausage,
    chopped
1 red pepper, cored,
    seeded and
    shredded
4 tomatoes, quartered
1 tablespoon chopped
    parsley
salt and pepper
4 eggs
TO SERVE:
4 tablespoons single
    cream
cayenne pepper or
    Tabasco

Heat the oil and butter in a pan, add the potatoes and sausage and fry quickly until lightly browned, shaking the pan to prevent the potato sticking. Add the pepper and tomatoes and cook for 3 to 4 minutes.

Remove from the heat and stir in the parsley, and salt and pepper to taste. Transfer to one large or 4 small buttered ovenproof dishes. Break the eggs on top and season lightly with salt and pepper.

Bake in a preheated moderate oven, 160°C (325°F), Gas Mark 3, for 15 to 20 minutes, until the eggs are just set.

Pour over the cream and sprinkle very lightly with cayenne pepper or Tabasco. Serve hot, with crusty bread, for lunch or supper.
Serves 4

Curried Eggs

8 eggs (size 1)
2 tablespoons oil
2 onions, chopped
2 cloves garlic,
    crushed
2.5 cm (1 inch) piece
    root ginger, chopped,
    or ½ teaspoon
    ground ginger
½ teaspoon ground
    cinnamon
1 teaspoon paprika
1 teaspoon salt
1 tablespoon mild
    curry powder
2 tablespoons
    desiccated coconut
6 tablespoons
    pineapple juice
300 ml (½ pint)
    chicken stock
300 g (10.4 oz)
    natural yogurt
1 tablespoon garam
    masala (optional)

Place the eggs in a saucepan and cover completely with water. Bring to the boil over moderate heat and boil gently for 5 minutes.

Meanwhile, heat the oil in a heavy-based pan. Add the onions, garlic and root ginger, if using, and fry quickly for 3 minutes, stirring. Add the ground ginger, if using, cinnamon, paprika, salt and curry powder. Cook gently for about 10 minutes, stirring occasionally.

Meanwhile, shell the eggs and add to the onion mixture with the coconut, pineapple juice, stock and yogurt. Heat slowly until simmering and simmer for 20 minutes. Stir in the garam masala, if using, and simmer for a further 2 to 3 minutes.

Serve hot with boiled rice and side dishes of onion and tomato salad, toasted coconut, thinly sliced cucumber in natural yogurt, sliced banana in lemon juice, and chutneys.
Serves 4

Smoked Mackerel Kedgeree

3 hard-boiled eggs
250 g (8 oz) smoked
    mackerel fillet,
    flaked
175 g (6 oz) long-
    grain rice, cooked
40 g (1½ oz) butter
2 tablespoons single
    cream (optional)
1 tablespoon chopped
    parsley
1 tablespoon lemon
    juice
salt and pepper
TO GARNISH:
paprika
3–4 watercress sprigs

Separate one egg yolk from the white
and keep on one side for garnish.
Chop the white with the other eggs.

Combine the chopped eggs with
the other ingredients in a large
saucepan, adding salt and pepper to
taste. Cover and heat gently for 3 to 4
minutes, shaking occasionally, until
thoroughly heated. Transfer to a
warmed serving dish.

Sieve the reserved yolk over the
top and garnish with paprika and
watercress. Serve hot.
Serves 4

Scotch Woodcock

4 thin slices hot
   buttered toast
1 × 35 g (1 oz) jar
   anchovy paste
3–4 eggs
25 g (1 oz) butter
mustard and cress to
   garnish

Spread the toast with the anchovy paste. Lightly scramble the eggs with the butter (see page 7) and place on the anchovy toasts. Garnish with mustard and cress.
Serve immediately.
Serves 2

Welsh Rarebit

250 g (8 oz) matured
   Cheddar cheese,
   grated
150 ml (¼ pint)
   brown ale
2 egg yolks
40 g (1½ oz) butter
¼ teaspoon salt
¼ teaspoon pepper
dash of Worcester-
   shire sauce
TO SERVE:
4 thick slices of toast
cayenne pepper

Place the ingredients in a heavy-based pan. Heat gently, stirring occasionally, until smooth, creamy and hot; do *not* boil.
   Place the toast on individual warmed serving plates. Pour the cheese mixture over, sprinkle with cayenne and serve immediately.
Serves 4

Golden Buck Rarebit: Use 2 whole eggs instead of yolks. Use flameproof plates and brown under a very hot grill for 1 minute, before serving.
Swiss Rarebit: Replace the Cheddar with Gruyère, brown ale with single cream, and Worcestershire sauce with ¼ teaspoon grated nutmeg.

Croque-Monsieur

4 thick slices buttered
   bread
125–175 g (4–6 oz)
   Cheddar cheese,
   sliced
4 tomatoes, sliced
4 rashers streaky
   bacon, derinded
   and halved
4 fried eggs

Place the bread buttered side up in a shallow flameproof dish or on individual flameproof plates and toast under a hot grill until golden brown. Cover completely with the cheese and grill until just melted.
   Place the tomato slices on top, stretch the halved bacon rashers with the back of a knife until very thin and place 2 on each slice of bread. Grill until the bacon is crisp. Top with a fried egg and serve immediately.
Serves 4

Onion Tart

PASTRY:
250 g (8 oz) plain
    flour
1/2 teaspoon salt
50 g (2 oz) butter or
    margarine
50 g (2 oz) lard
1–2 tablespoons
    water

FILLING:
50 g (2 oz) butter
750 g (1 1/2 lb)
    onions, sliced
125 g (4 oz) very fat
    smoked bacon,
    derinded and
    chopped
25 g (1 oz) plain
    flour
142 ml (5 fl oz)
    soured cream
3 eggs, lightly beaten
1/2 teaspoon salt
1/2 teaspoon pepper

Make the pastry and line a 23 cm (9 inch) flan dish or ring as for Quiche Lorraine (see opposite).

To make the filling, melt the butter in a pan, add the onions and bacon and fry until soft and golden but not browned. Remove from the heat and stir in the remaining ingredients.

Pour into the prepared flan case and smooth the top. Bake in a preheated moderately hot oven, 200°C (400°F), Gas Mark 6, for 35 to 40 minutes, until set and golden brown. Serve hot, with a salad.
Serves 6

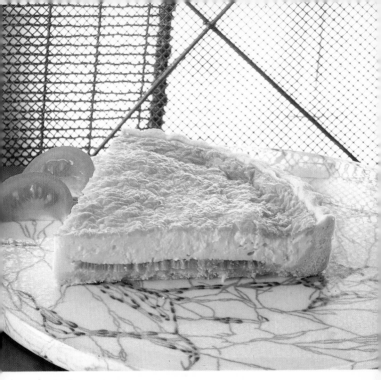

Quiche Lorraine

PASTRY:
250 g (8 oz) plain
  flour
1/2 teaspoon salt
150 g (5 oz) butter or
  margarine
1–1 1/2 tablespoons
  water

FILLING:
250 g (8 oz) thinly
  sliced back bacon,
  derinded
3 eggs
142 ml (5 fl oz)
  double cream
pepper

Sift the flour and salt into a bowl.
Rub in the fat until the mixture
resembles fine breadcrumbs. Add the
water and mix to a firm dough.
Knead lightly until smooth. Wrap in
cling film or polythene and chill for
15 to 20 minutes.

Roll the pastry into a round on a
lightly floured surface and use to line
a 23 cm (9 inch) flan dish or ring.
Trim off any excess pastry and prick
the base well with a fork. If possible,
chill the flan case for a further 20 to 30
minutes.

Line the pastry case with the bacon
rashers and bake on the top shelf of a
preheated moderately hot oven,
200°C (400°F), Gas Mark 6, for
10 minutes. Lightly whisk together
the eggs and cream, adding pepper to
taste. Pour over the bacon and return
to the oven for 25 to 30 minutes, until
set and golden brown. Serve hot.
Serves 6

Cheese and Onion Pudding

50 g (2 oz) butter
6 thin slices bread
175 g (6 oz) Cheddar
    cheese, grated
1 onion, chopped
4 eggs
284 ml (½ pint)
    single or half cream
300 ml (½ pint) milk
½ teaspoon dried
    mustard
dash of Tabasco
    (optional)
salt and pepper

Spread most of the butter onto the bread. Cut each slice into 16 squares. Use remaining butter to grease a 1.5 litre (2½ pint) casserole.

Layer the bread, cheese and onion in the dish, finishing with a layer of cheese. Whisk eggs with remaining ingredients, adding salt and pepper to taste. Pour into the dish and set aside for 10 minutes.

Bake on the top shelf of a preheated moderately hot oven, 200°C (400°F), Gas Mark 6, for 30 minutes, or until set and golden brown and slightly puffed up. Serve immediately.
Serves 4

Bacon and Egg Pie

CHEESE PASTRY:
175 g (6 oz) plain
    flour
½ teaspoon dried
    mustard
¼ teaspoon salt
75 g (3 oz) butter or
    margarine, cut into
    small pieces
40 g (1½ oz)
    Cheddar cheese,
    finely grated
1 egg yolk
3 teaspoons water
FILLING:
8–10 rashers streaky
    bacon, derinded,
    stretched and
    halved
6 eggs (size 4 or 5),
    separated

Sift the flour, mustard and salt into a bowl. Rub in the fat until the mixture resembles fine breadcrumbs. Stir in the cheese, then add the egg yolk and water and mix to a firm dough. Knead until smooth and chill for 15 to 20 minutes.

Roll out two thirds of the pastry on a floured surface and use to line a 20 cm (8 inch) flan dish. Roll the remaining pastry into a lid. Grill the bacon until beginning to crisp; cool. Whisk the egg whites until just stiff enough to hold their shape. Place half the bacon in the pastry case. Spoon two thirds of the egg white on top and make 6 hollows with the back of a spoon. Drop an egg yolk into each hollow and cover with the remaining egg white and bacon.

Cover with the lid, seal and flute the edge and make a slit in the centre. Bake in a preheated moderately hot oven, 200°C (400°F), Gas Mark 6, for 25 to 30 minutes. Serve immediately.
Serves 6

Egg and Sardine Jalousie

1 × 370 g (13 oz)
  packet frozen puff
  pastry, thawed
4 hard-boiled eggs,
  chopped
1 × 120 g (4¼ oz)
  can sardines in oil,
  drained
1–2 teaspoons curry
  powder
1 tablespoon chopped
  parsley
4 tablespoons
  mayonnaise or
  salad cream
salt and pepper
beaten egg to glaze

Roll the pastry into a 30 cm (12 inch) square, then cut in half. Place one piece on a baking sheet.

Mix together the remaining ingredients, adding salt and pepper to taste. Spread over the pastry on the baking sheet, leaving a 1 cm (½ inch) border around the edge. Brush the edges with water and place the remaining pastry on top. Seal and flute the edges; brush with beaten egg. Decorate with shapes cut from the trimmings. Make cuts across the top about 5 mm (¼ inch) apart.

Bake on the top shelf of a preheated hot oven, 220°C (425°F), Gas Mark 7, for 15 minutes. Serve hot.

Serves 4

CRÈMES, PUDDINGS & PIES

Ratafia Crème Brulée

6 egg yolks
2 × 284 ml (½ pint)
  cartons double
  cream
½ teaspoon almond
  essence
1 × 85 g (3 oz)
  packet ratafia
  biscuits, finely
  crushed
75 g (3 oz) caster
  sugar

Whisk the egg yolks in a bowl. Heat the cream gently to just below boiling point and stir into the egg yolks. Place the bowl over a pan of simmering water or pour the cream mixture into the top of a double saucepan. Heat gently until the mixture thickens, but do not boil.

When the mixture is thick enough to coat the back of a spoon, remove from the heat and stir in the essence. Pour into 6 or 8 ramekin dishes. Cool, then chill overnight.

Cover with the crushed ratafias, then with sugar. Place under a moderately hot grill until the sugar melts and caramelizes. Cool, then chill for 2 to 3 hours before serving.
Serves 6 or 8

Coffee Crème Caramel

75 g (3 oz)
   granulated sugar
1 tablespoon water
3 eggs
25 g (1 oz) caster
   sugar
450 ml (¾ pint) milk
1 tablespoon instant
   coffee powder

Place the granulated sugar and water in a small heavy-based pan. Heat gently until the sugar has completely dissolved. Increase the heat and boil rapidly until a deep brown caramel forms. Pour immediately into 8 buttered ramekin dishes, or a 900 ml (1½ pint) mould. Leave to cool.

Whisk the eggs and caster sugar in a bowl. Heat the milk until warm, stir in the coffee powder and whisk into the eggs. Strain and pour into the moulds. Place in a roasting pan containing enough warm water to come almost to the top of the dishes.

Bake in a preheated moderate oven, 160°C (325°F), Gas Mark 3, for 40 to 45 minutes for individual crème caramels, about 1 hour for a large one, or until set.

Leave until cold then turn onto a serving dish(es). Serve with cream.
Serves 4 or 8

Key Lime Pie

50 g (2 oz) soft light brown sugar
175 g (6 oz) digestive biscuits, crushed
50 g (2 oz) butter, melted
grated rind and juice of 3 limes
1 envelope gelatine, dissolved in 2 tablespoons water
2 eggs, separated
few drops of green food colouring (optional)
1 × 397 g (14 oz) can condensed milk
TO DECORATE:
1 lime, thinly sliced
whipped cream

Stir the sugar and biscuit crumbs into the melted butter until well mixed. Turn into a 20 cm (8 inch) pie dish or loose-bottomed flan tin and press evenly over the bottom and sides. Chill well.

Add the lime juice to the dissolved gelatine, then whisk in the grated rind, egg yolks and colouring (if using). Gradually whisk in the condensed milk. Leave until just beginning to set, stirring occasionally.

Whisk the egg whites until really stiff and fold into the lime mixture. Turn into the crumb case and chill for several hours.

Decorate with lime slices and piped cream rosettes.
Serves 6

Vanilla Rice Creams

50 g (2 oz) round-grain rice
450 ml (¾ pint) milk
50 g (2 oz) sugar
2 eggs, separated
1 teaspoon vanilla essence
142 ml (5 fl oz) whipping cream, whipped
TO DECORATE:
25 g (1 oz) crunch nut topping

Place the rice in a heavy-based pan. Add the milk and sugar and bring to the boil, stirring constantly. Cover and cook over very low heat for 40 to 45 minutes, stirring occasionally, until all the milk has been absorbed and the rice is soft.

Beat in the egg yolks, one at a time, and return to the heat for 1 minute, without boiling, stirring constantly. Beat in the vanilla essence. Sieve or work in an electric blender or food processor until smooth; cool.

Whisk the egg whites until stiff. Fold together the egg whites, rice mixture and cream. Spoon into individual serving dishes and chill.

Sprinkle with nut topping to serve.
Serves 6
NOTE: For a speedy version, heat 1 × 435 g (15.5 oz) can creamed rice, then beat in the egg yolks and proceed as above.

Chocolate Fudge Pudding

FUDGE TOPPING:
40 g (1½ oz) butter
40 g (1½ oz) soft dark brown sugar
40 g (1½ oz) golden syrup
15 g (½ oz) cocoa powder
2 tablespoons single or half cream
50 g (2 oz) walnuts or pecans, finely chopped

CAKE MIXTURE:
2 eggs
125 g (4 oz) caster sugar
125 g (4 oz) butter or margarine
125 g (4 oz) self-raising flour
1 teaspoon baking powder

Place all the fudge ingredients in a small heavy-based pan. Heat gently until boiling, stirring constantly, and boil for 30 seconds. Pour into a base-lined and greased 20 cm (8 inch) sandwich tin, or a well greased 1.5 litre (2½ pint) ring mould. Leave until cold.

Place the cake mixture ingredients in a large mixing bowl and beat with a wooden spoon for 2 minutes. Turn onto the cooled fudge mixture and spread evenly with a palette knife.

Bake in a preheated moderate oven, 160°C (325°F), Gas Mark 3, for 40 to 45 minutes, until well risen, golden brown and firm to the touch. Leave in the tin for 5 minutes.

Invert onto a serving plate and peel off the lining paper. The fudge mixture now becomes a soft, sticky topping which will run down the sides.

Serve hot with cream or Vanilla Cream Sauce (see page 92).
Serves 6 to 8

Ginger Queen of Puddings

600 ml (1 pint) milk
pared rind of
  ½ lemon
50 g (2 oz) butter
175 g (6 oz) caster
  sugar
75 g (3 oz) fine fresh
  white breadcrumbs
3 eggs, separated
3–4 tablespoons
  ginger marmalade

Place the milk and lemon rind in a pan over a very low heat and leave to infuse for 10 minutes. Discard the lemon rind.

Add the butter and 50 g (2 oz) of the sugar to the milk and stir until melted. Add the breadcrumbs and egg yolks and mix well. Transfer to a well-buttered shallow 1.2 litre (2 pint) ovenproof dish.

Leave to stand for 10 to 15 minutes then bake in a preheated moderate oven, 180°C (350°F), Gas Mark 4, for 15 to 20 minutes or until set. Cool slightly, then spread with the marmalade.

Whisk the egg whites until stiff. Whisk in half the remaining sugar, then fold in all but 2 teaspoons of the rest. Pipe or spoon the meringue over the baked pudding and sprinkle with the reserved sugar. Return to a cool oven, 150°C (300°F), Gas Mark 2, for 8 to 10 minutes, until golden brown.

Serve warm.

Serves 6

Burnt Cream Banana Pie

**SHORTBREAD
  DOUGH:**
*150 g (5 oz) plain
  flour*
75 g (3 oz) butter
*40 g (1½ oz) caster
  sugar*

FILLING:
*1½ tablespoons
  cornflour*
300 ml (½ pint) milk
*4 tablespoons single
  cream*
4 egg yolks
*15 g (½ oz) caster
  sugar*
*½ teaspoon vanilla
  essence*
1–2 bananas

TOPPING:
*175 g (6 oz) caster or
  demerara sugar*
*banana slices to
  decorate*

Sift the flour into a bowl. Add the butter and sugar and rub in until the mixture resembles breadcrumbs. Press the mixture together into a stiff dough. Knead on a lightly floured surface until smooth.

Place in the centre of a 20 cm (8 inch) flan dish and press with the knuckles until the dough completely covers the base. Prick well and bake on the top shelf of a preheated cool oven, 150°C (300°F), Gas Mark 2, for about 40 minutes, until pale golden and set. Cool in the dish.

Blend the cornflour with the milk in a pan. Bring slowly to the boil, stirring, until thickened. Lower the heat to a minimum. Beat in the cream, egg yolks, sugar and vanilla and heat for 2 to 3 minutes, stirring; do not boil. Cool slightly.

Slice the bananas and arrange over the shortbread base. Cover immediately with the egg custard and chill until set, preferably overnight.

Sprinkle the sugar evenly over the top. Place under a hot grill until the sugar melts and caramelizes. Chill for 2 to 3 hours before serving, decorated with banana slices.
Serves 6 to 8

Baked Cinnamon Cheesecake

shortbread dough
  (see recipe)
1 × 227 g (8 oz)
  packet creamy soft
  cheese
227 g (8 oz) curd
  cheese
50 g (2 oz) soft light
  brown sugar
142 ml (5 fl oz)
  soured cream
2 teaspoons ground
  cinnamon
4 eggs
TO DECORATE:
3–4 tablespoons
  double cream,
  whipped
ground cinnamon

Make the shortbread dough as for opposite recipe, increasing the flour to 175 g (6 oz), the butter to 125 g (4 oz) and the sugar to 50 g (2 oz).

Soften the cream cheese in a bowl. Beat in the curd cheese and sugar, then stir in the cream and cinnamon. Whisk in the eggs, one at a time.

Place the shortbread in a lined and greased deep 20 cm (8 inch) loose-bottomed cake tin. Press firmly with the knuckles to cover the base and sides completely.

Pour in the cheese mixture. Bake in a preheated moderate oven, 160°C (325°F), Gas Mark 3, for 1 hour, until set. Leave in the tin until cold.

Transfer to a serving plate and decorate with piped cream rosettes. Sprinkle lightly with cinnamon.
Serves 8

Pecan Pie

SHORTCRUST
   PASTRY:
*175 g (6 oz) plain
   flour*
125 g (4 oz) butter
1 egg yolk
*2–3 teaspoons cold
   water*
FILLING:
25 g (1 oz) butter
*125 g (4 oz) caster
   sugar*
*175 g (6 oz) maple or
   golden syrup*
4 eggs (size 1 or 2)
*1 teaspoon vanilla
   essence*
*50 g (2 oz) Pecan
   nuts or walnuts,
   chopped*

Sift the flour into a mixing bowl. Rub in the butter until the mixture resembles breadcrumbs. Add the egg yolk and water and mix to a firm dough. Knead lightly on a floured surface until smooth. Roll out and use to line a 20 cm (8 inch) fluted flan ring or pie dish. If possible, chill for 20 to 30 minutes.

Line with greaseproof paper and dried beans and bake blind on the top shelf of a preheated moderately hot oven, 200°C (400°F), Gas Mark 6, for 15 to 20 minutes. Remove the beans and paper and return to the oven for 5 minutes. Cool and remove the flan ring, if used.

Cream the butter and sugar until very soft and creamy. Gradually beat in the syrup, then beat in the eggs, one at a time, and vanilla essence (the mixture may look curdled). Pour into the pastry case and sprinkle the nuts on top.

Bake in a preheated hot oven, 220°C (425°F), Gas Mark 7, for 10 minutes, then lower the temperature to 180°C (350°F), Gas Mark 4, and cook for 30 to 35 minutes. Serve cool, with whipped cream if desired.
Serves 6 to 8

Baked Custard Tart

*shortcrust pastry
   made with 175 g
   (6 oz) flour (see
   recipe above)*
4 eggs
*25 g (1 oz) caster
   sugar*
*½ teaspoon vanilla
   essence*
450 ml (¾ pint) milk
grated nutmeg

Prepare and cook a 20 cm (8 inch) flan case as for Pecan Pie.

Lightly whisk the eggs with the sugar and vanilla essence in a bowl. Heat the milk until warm and whisk in the eggs. Strain into the flan case and sprinkle with nutmeg.

Bake in a preheated moderate oven, 160°C (325°F), Gas Mark 3, for 45 to 50 minutes, until set and lightly browned. Serve warm or cold.
Serves 6

MERINGUES & COLD DESSERTS

Meringue is made from a mixture of whisked egg white and sugar. There are three types of meringue: meringue Suisse, meringue cuite and meringue Italienne. All three types are quite different, as the following recipes show, but there are some general basic rules.

All meringues should be prepared in a large, very clean, dry mixing bowl to allow the free movement of the egg white. This enables the maximum amount of air to be incorporated to produce the greatest increase in volume. Any grease or egg yolk will prevent the egg white from whisking. The egg whites should be at room temperature.

Although an electric or hand rotary whisk are much quicker to use, the best results are achieved with a wire balloon whisk or spiral whisk.

Meringue Suisse is the easiest and most frequently prepared meringue, simply made by whisking in 50 g (2 oz) caster sugar to each egg white. It does, however, deteriorate fairly quickly after preparation and should be used immediately, whereas meringue cuite and meringue Italienne hold their shape for several hours after preparation.

Meringues are best cooked on silicone or rice paper, but if neither is available use thoroughly oiled baking sheets.

Meringue Suisse

4 egg whites
250 g (8 oz) caster
  sugar
1 teaspoon lemon
  juice

Whisk the egg whites in a large bowl until very stiff and dry; if the meringue slides around the bowl when tilted, carry on whisking.

When the egg whites are stiff enough, add the sugar 1 tablespoon at a time, whisking very thoroughly between each addition. Finally, whisk in the lemon juice. The meringue should be glossy and form soft peaks.

For a more open-textured meringue, whisk in half the sugar and fold in the remainder with a wire whisk or metal spoon.

Use immediately to make shells, rounds or baskets; on pies and puddings; in mousses and ice creams.

This quantity will make:
about 72 × 2.5 cm (1 inch) shells;
8 to 12 × 7.5 cm (3 inch) baskets;
1 × 20 cm (8 inch) basket, vacherin or Pavlova circle;
3 × 20 cm (8 inch) flat circles.

Meringue Italienne

3 tablespoons water
250 g (8 oz)
    granulated sugar
3 egg whites,
    whisked
½ teaspoon vanilla
    essence

Place the water and sugar in a heavy-based pan over low heat until the sugar has dissolved and the liquid is clear. Increase the heat and boil rapidly until 150°C (298°F) registers on a sugar thermometer, or until a small amount, dropped into cold water, can be rolled into a hard ball.

Pour the syrup into the stiffly whisked egg whites in a slow thin stream, whisking constantly, to form a thick glossy meringue. Whisk in the vanilla essence.

Meringue Italienne is similar to an American frosting and should have the consistency of whipped cream. Use as a cake filling or topping, or on trifles.

This quantity is sufficient to fill and ice the top of a 20 cm (8 inch) cake.

Meringue Cuite

4 egg whites
250 g (8 oz) icing
  sugar, sifted
½ teaspoon vanilla
  essence

Place the ingredients in a large mixing bowl over a pan of simmering water. Whisk with a rotary or wire whisk for about 10 minutes, until the mixture is very thick and glossy and forms soft but well-shaped peaks.

Remove the bowl from the heat and continue whisking until the bowl is cool enough to touch; the heat from the bowl may crystallize the sugar.

Meringue cuite gives a much more defined shape than Meringue Suisse and retains its shape much longer.

Use as for Meringue Suisse (see page 81); quantities are the same.

Croquembouche

MERINGUE SHELLS:
4 egg whites
250 g (8 oz) caster
  sugar
1 teaspoon lemon
  juice
caster sugar for
  sprinkling
FILLING:
284 ml (½ pint)
  whipping cream
1 tablespoon kirsch
  (optional)
250 g (8 oz) black
  cherries, stoned

Prepare the meringue as for Meringue Suisse (see page 81). Using a large piping bag fitted with a 1 cm (½ inch) plain or star nozzle and baking sheets lined with silicone paper, pipe one third into shells about 2.5 cm (1 inch), a third slightly larger, and a third into shells about 3.5 cm (1½ inches). There should be about 16 of each size. Sprinkle lightly with sugar.

Place in a very cool oven, 120°C (250°F), Gas Mark ½, for 2 hours or until firm. Remove the paper, turn upside down and return to the oven for 1 to 1½ hours to dry.

Whip the cream with the kirsch, if using, until stiff. Spoon into a piping bag fitted with a star nozzle.

Arrange some of the larger meringue shells in a 20 cm (8 inch) circle on a serving plate. Pipe a rosette of cream between each. Arrange the remaining shells, with the cherries in between, on top in progressively smaller circles to form a pyramid, using rosettes of cream to hold the shape.
Serves 6

St. Valentine's Vacherin

MERINGUE BASKET:
4 egg whites
250 g (8 oz) icing
  sugar, sifted
½ teaspoon vanilla
  essence
FILLING:
284 ml (½ pint)
  whipping cream,
  whipped
340 g (12 oz) fresh or
  frozen raspberries,
  thawed
3 tablespoons
  raspberry conserve,
  sieved and warmed
TOPPING:
icing sugar for
  sprinkling

Line a baking sheet with silicone paper. Mark a large heart shape on the paper, about 20 cm (8 inches) wide and 23 cm (9 inches) long.

Prepare the meringue as for Meringue Cuite (see page 83) and spoon into a large piping bag fitted with a 1 cm (½ inch) star nozzle. Pipe around the outline of the heart then fill in the middle. Pipe large rosettes or swirls around the edge, making a heart-shaped basket.

Place in a very cool oven, 110°C (225°F), Gas Mark ¼, for 4 to 5 hours or until the meringue is completely dry. For a really white meringue, leave in the oven overnight with the door slightly open.

Very carefully lift the meringue basket onto a flat serving dish. Spread the cream over the base, top with raspberries and spoon over the warm conserve.

Sprinkle lightly with icing sugar to serve.
Serves 6

Baked Alaska

1 × 15–18 cm (6–7
  inch) sponge flan
  case
250 g (8 oz)
  strawberries, sliced
  (optional)
$^1/_3$–$^1/_2$ litre
  ($^3/_4$–1 pint) straw-
  berry ice cream

MERINGUE TOPPING:
4 egg whites
250 g (8 oz) caster
  sugar
$^1/_2$ teaspoon vanilla
  essence

TO DECORATE:
25–50 g (1–2 oz)
  flaked almonds
  (optional)
caster sugar

Place the flan case on an ovenproof
plate and arrange the strawberries on
the base, if using. Spoon the ice
cream over the top. Place in the
freezer or freezing compartment of
the refrigerator while making the
meringue topping, as in Meringue
Suisse (see page 81).

Working as quickly as possible,
pile the meringue onto the prepared
base, completely enclosing the ice
cream. Stick the almonds into the
meringue, if using, and sprinkle
lightly with a little caster sugar. Place
immediately in a preheated hot oven,
200°C (400°F), Gas Mark 6, for 3 to 4
minutes or until the meringue peaks
are lightly browned. Serve
immediately.
Serves 6

Italian-style Trifle

4 trifle sponges
2 tablespoons sherry
  (optional)
1 × 439 g (15½ oz)
  can pineapple
  pieces
300 ml (½ pint) cold
  Vanilla Cream
  Sauce (see page 92)
MERINGUE TOPPING:
3 egg whites
175 g (6 oz) caster
  sugar
½ teaspoon vanilla
  essence

Crumble the trifle sponges into an
ovenproof serving dish. Sprinkle
with the sherry, if using. Drain the
pineapple and sprinkle half of the
juice over the cake. Arrange the
pineapple pieces on top and pour over
the vanilla sauce.

Prepare the meringue as for
Meringue Suisse (see page 81) and
spoon over the sauce. Place in a
preheated moderately hot oven,
200°C (400°F), Gas Mark 6, for 3 to 4
minutes until just the tips of the
meringue are golden brown.

Serve warm or cold.
Serves 6 to 8

Pineapple Meringue Pie

shortcrust pastry
  made with 175 g
  (6 oz) flour (see
  Pecan Pie, page
  78)
50 g (2 oz) cornflour
450 ml (¾ pint)
  pineapple juice
3 eggs, separated
25 g (1 oz) butter
175 g (6 oz) caster
  sugar
caster sugar for
  sprinkling

Roll out the pastry and use to line a
20 cm (8 inch) fluted flan dish or flan
ring. Bake blind as for Pecan Pie
(page 78).

Blend the cornflour with a little of
the pineapple juice in a pan.

Add the remaining juice and heat
slowly, stirring, until thickened.
Remove from the heat and beat in the
egg yolks and butter. Pour into the
pastry case and cool.

Whisk the egg whites until very
stiff and dry. Add the sugar a little at
a time, whisking thoroughly between
each addition until the meringue is
glossy and forms soft peaks.

Spoon into a large piping bag fitted
with a 1 cm (½ inch) star nozzle and
pipe over the pineapple filling.
Sprinkle lightly with a little caster
sugar.

Bake in a preheated moderate
oven, 160°C (325°F), Gas Mark 3, for
15 to 20 minutes, until golden brown.
Serve warm or cold.
Serves 6

Chocolate Mint Ice Cream

25 g (1 oz) custard
    powder
300 ml (½ pint) milk
1 × 170 g (6 oz) can
    evaporated milk
2 eggs, separated
40 g (1½ oz) icing
    sugar
25 g (1 oz) butter
½ teaspoon
    peppermint
    flavouring
½ teaspoon green
    food colouring
TOPPING:
50 g (2 oz) chocolate,
    melted and cooled
2 tablespoons single
    cream
TO DECORATE:
3–4 tablespoons
    double cream,
    whipped

Blend the custard powder with
2 tablespoons milk in a large bowl.
Heat the remaining milk and
evaporated milk until boiling and
stir into the mixture. Return to the
pan and heat, stirring, until very
thick.

Return to the bowl and beat in the
egg yolks, one at a time. Beat in the
icing sugar, butter, flavouring and
colouring and set aside until cold,
whisking occasionally.

Whisk the egg whites until very
stiff and fold into the cold custard.
Transfer to a rigid freezerproof
container, cover and freeze for about
1 hour, until beginning to freeze.
Whisk well, re-cover and partially
freeze again. Repeat the process at
least twice.

Spoon into individual freezerproof
dishes. Cover and freeze until firm.

Combine the chocolate and cream
and spoon over the ice cream.
Decorate with piped cream.
Serves 4 to 6

Ginger Snap Ice Cream

3 eggs, separated
50 g (2 oz) soft dark
  brown sugar
4 tablespoons green
  ginger wine
50 g (2 oz) butter,
  melted
150 g (5 oz) ginger
  biscuits, finely
  crushed
284 ml (½ pint)
  double cream

Place the egg yolks in a mixing bowl over a pan of hot water. Add the sugar and half the ginger wine and whisk until pale and creamy. Remove from the heat and whisk until cool. Stir in 1 tablespoon of the remaining ginger wine, the melted butter and all but 25 g (1 oz) of the biscuit crumbs.

Whisk the cream and egg whites together until stiff enough to form soft peaks. Whisk in the remaining ginger wine. Fold both mixtures together and transfer to a rigid freezerproof container. Cover with clingfilm and freeze for about 1 hour, until just beginning to freeze around the edge. Whisk well, re-cover and partially freeze again. Repeat the process at least twice more. Cover, seal and freeze until firm.

Transfer to the refrigerator 30 minutes before serving. Scoop into chilled glasses and sprinkle with the remaining biscuit crumbs.
Serves 6 to 8

Orange Curaçao Cheesecake

50 g (2 oz) butter
50 g (2 oz) soft dark
   brown sugar
175 g (6 oz) digestive
   biscuits, crushed
1 × 227 g (8 oz)
   packet creamy soft
   cheese
227 g (8 oz) curd
   cheese
2 eggs, separated
142 ml (5 fl oz)
   soured cream
25 g (1 oz) caster
   sugar
grated rind and juice
   of 1 orange
1 envelope gelatine,
   dissolved in
   2 tablespoons water
2–3 tablespoons
   orange Curaçao
TO DECORATE:
142 ml (5 fl oz)
   double cream
½ orange, sliced

Melt the butter and stir in the brown sugar and biscuit crumbs. Press onto the base of a 23 cm (9 inch) loose-bottomed flan tin or cake tin. Chill until firm.

Mix together the cheeses in a mixing bowl, then beat in the egg yolks, soured cream and caster sugar. Stir in the orange rind and juice, dissolved gelatine and Curaçao. Leave until just on the point of setting, then fold in the stiffly whisked egg whites.

Pour onto the biscuit base and chill until firm. Decorate with piped whipped cream and orange slices.
Serves 6 to 8

Grapefruit Sorbet

2 grapefruit
   (preferably pink)
1 envelope gelatine,
   dissolved in
   2 tablespoons
   water
600 ml (1 pint)
   grapefruit juice
25 g (1 oz) caster
   sugar
150 g (5.2 oz)
   natural yogurt
2 egg whites, stiffly
   beaten
8 mint sprigs to
   decorate

Finely grate the rind from both grapefruits. Place in a large bowl and add just enough boiling water to cover. Leave to soak for 5 minutes, then drain.

Cut the grapefruits in half and squeeze thoroughly so that the flesh comes out with the juice. Add to the soaked rind, together with the dissolved gelatine, grapefruit juice, sugar and yogurt. Stir well, then transfer to a rigid freezerproof container, cover with clingfilm and freeze for about 1 hour, until just beginning to freeze around the edge. Whisk, then fold in the egg whites. Partly freeze and whisk twice more. Cover, seal and freeze until firm.

Transfer to the refrigerator 10 minutes before serving to soften. Scoop into chilled glasses and decorate with mint sprigs.
Serves 8

SAUCES

Mayonnaise

2 egg yolks
1 teaspoon lemon
  juice
1/4 teaspoon pepper
1/4 teaspoon French
  mustard
1/4 teaspoon caster
  sugar
300 ml (1/2 pint)
  olive oil or corn oil
1–2 tablespoons
  white wine vinegar
1/4 teaspoon salt

Blend the egg yolks, lemon juice, pepper, mustard and sugar in a bowl. Alternatively, work in an electric blender or food processor.

Add about a third of the oil, a drop at a time, beating thoroughly between each addition. Stir in 2 teaspoons of the vinegar.

Continue adding the oil, a drop at a time. As the mayonnaise thickens, increase the flow of oil to a slow steady stream, beating constantly.

When all the oil has been added, beat in enough vinegar to give the required flavour and thickness, and season with salt.

If, at any time the mayonnaise curdles, place one egg yolk in a clean bowl and add the curdled mixture as if it were oil.
Makes about 450 ml (3/4 pint)

Aioli: Crush 3 cloves garlic and add to egg yolks with seasonings.
Sauce Indienne: To the prepared mayonnaise, add 1 tablespoon mild curry powder and 1 tablespoon chopped chives or finely chopped spring onion.

Vanilla Cream Sauce

3 egg yolks
15 g (1/2 oz) caster
  sugar
300 ml (1/2 pint) milk
7.5 cm (3 inch) piece
  of vanilla pod,
  split, or
  1/2 teaspoon
  vanilla essence

Blend the egg yolks with the sugar in a small bowl. Heat the milk with the vanilla pod, if using, until boiling. Discard the vanilla pod and pour the milk onto the egg yolks, stirring.

Return to the pan and heat very gently, stirring, until thick enough to coat the back of a spoon; do not boil. Stir in the vanilla essence, if using; strain into a jug. Serve hot or cold.
Makes 300 ml (1/2 pint)

Sauce Suprême

25 g (1 oz) butter
25 g (1 oz) flour
450 ml (¾ pint)
  well-flavoured
  chicken stock
1 teaspoon lemon
  juice
3–4 egg yolks
3–4 tablespoons
  double cream
salt and pepper

Melt the butter in a pan, stir in the flour and cook, stirring, until golden. Remove from the heat and gradually stir in the stock. Bring to the boil, stirring, until thickened. Simmer for about 5 minutes, stirring. Pour into the top of a double saucepan or a bowl over a pan of simmering water.

Blend together the lemon juice, egg yolks, cream, and a little salt and pepper, and stir into the sauce. Heat gently, stirring very frequently, until thickened; do not boil. Check the seasoning and use the sauce as required, e.g. for chicken fricassée or blanquette.

Makes about 450 ml (¾ pint)

Hollandaise Sauce

3 tablespoons white
  wine vinegar
1 small bay leaf
1 small blade mace,
  or pinch of ground
  mace or nutmeg
3 peppercorns
2 egg yolks
¼ teaspoon salt
about 125 g (4 oz)
  butter, softened

Pour the vinegar into a small saucepan. Add the bay leaf, mace or nutmeg and peppercorns. Boil until the vinegar has reduced to about 2 teaspoons. Strain into a clean small bowl over a pan of very gently simmering water. Stir in the egg yolks and salt.

Using a small wire whisk or wooden spoon, add the butter about 15 g (½ oz) at a time, beating very thoroughly between each addition until the mixture is smooth and thick enough to hold its shape. Remove from the heat and check the seasoning.

Serve warm rather than hot, with fish or vegetable dishes.

Makes about 200 ml (⅓ pint)

Mousseline Sauce: Whip 3 tablespoons double cream until stiff. Fold into the Hollandaise sauce and season with salt to taste. Serve immediately with poached or grilled fish, and with asparagus.

INDEX

Acknowledgments

Photography by Paul Williams
Food prepared by Caroline Ellwood
Photographic stylist: Penny Markham